ORTHO'S All About
Landscaping

Written by Jo Kellum, ASLA

Meredith® Books
Des Moines, Iowa

Ortho® Books
An imprint of Meredith® Books

Ortho's All About Landscaping
Editor: Michael McKinley
Art Director: Tom Wegner
Copy Chief: Catherine Hamrick
Copy and Production Editor: Terri Fredrickson
Contributing Editors: Martin Miller, Roberta J. Peterson
Contributing Technical Editor: Jeff Logsdon
Contributing Writer: Greg Henry Quinn
Contributing Proofreaders: Kathy Eastman, Gretchen
    Kaufmann, JoEllyn Witke
Contributing Illustrator: Pam Wattenmaker
Contributing Map Illustrator: Jana Fothergill
Contributing Prop/Photo Stylists: Mary E. Klingaman,
    Diane Munkel, Pamela K. Peirce
Indexer: Guy Cunningham
Electronic Production Coordinator: Paula Forest
Editorial and Design Assistants: Kathleen Stevens,
    Karen Schirm
Production Director: Douglas M. Johnston
Production Manager: Pam Kvitne
Assistant Prepress Manager: Marjorie J. Schenkelberg

Additional Editorial Contributions from
    Art Rep Services
Director: Chip Nadeau
Designer: lk Design
Illustrators: John Teisberg, Shawn Wallace

Meredith® Books
Editor in Chief: James D. Blume
Design Director: Matt Strelecki
Managing Editor: Gregory H. Kayko
Executive Ortho Editor: Benjamin W. Allen

Director, Sales & Marketing, Retail: Michael A. Peterson
Director, Sales & Marketing, Special Markets:
    Rita McMullen
Director, Sales & Marketing, Home & Garden Center
    Channel: Ray Wolf
Director, Operations: George A. Susral

Vice President, General Manager: Jamie L. Martin

Meredith Publishing Group
President, Publishing Group: Christopher M. Little
Vice President, Consumer Marketing & Development:
    Hal Oringer

Meredith Corporation
Chairman and Chief Executive Officer: William T. Kerr

Chairman of the Executive Committee: E.T. Meredith III

Cover photograph: Azaleas and dogwoods enframe a simple
yet inviting gravel entry path. Photograph by Susan Roth.

All of us at Ortho® Books are dedicated to providing you
with the information and ideas you need to enhance your
home and garden. We welcome your comments and
suggestions about this book. Write to us at:
    Meredith Corporation
    Ortho Books
    1716 Locust St.
    Des Moines, IA 50309–3023

Thanks to
Claire Anderson, Debra Anderson, Greg Anderson,
Juanita Chau, Jackie Donovan, Melissa George,
Colleen Johnson, Aaron McCann, Aimee Reiman,
Urban Farmer Store of San Francisco

Photographers
(Photographers credited may retain copyright ©
    to the listed photographs. Names in parentheses are
    landscape designers.)
L= Left, R= Right, C= Center, B= Bottom, T= Top
Bob Braun: 64BR; **Karen Bussolini/Positive Images:** 44B,
86TR; **Kennon Cooke/Valan Photos:** 45TL, 45BR;
Thomas E. Eltzroth: 73TR; **Richard P. Felber:** 5BC, 10TL
(William Fredricks), 10CR (Oehme, van Sweden), 10B
(Oehme, van Sweden), 12B (George Schoellkopf), 15TL,
18CL (Raymond Jungles), 19T (Oscar de la Renta), 19CL
(Oehme, van Sweden),, 20CL, 21TR (Hitch Layman),
21BL (Steve Martino), 21BR (Oehme, van Sweden), 23TL,
23TC, 41BC (Oehme, van Sweden), 44T, 46BL, 65TR
(Oehme, van Sweden), 74T (John Saladino), 75TR (John
Saladino), 75C, 85BR (Steve Martino), 89TR; **John
Glover:** 46TR; 48T (Julian Dowle), 64TL, 65TL, 73B, 74B,
75BR; **David Goldberg:** 66TL, 79TL,TR,BR, 80TL, 84BL,
84BR, 87TR, 87BR; **Jerry Harpur:** 8BL (Bruce Kelly), 8TR
(Keeyla Meadows), 9BR (Jim Matsuo), 14T, 16TL, 17CR,
19CR, 20BR, 23TR, 24TL, 24B, 25T, 41TL (Bruce Kelly),
43TR (Frank Cabot), 43BL (Bruce Kelly), 46BR, 47TR
(Fred Watson), 48C (Bob Dash), 48B (Sonny Garcia), 49C
(Mark Rios), 49B (Keeyla Meadows), 51 Row 1-3 (Jim
Matsuo), 51 Row1-4 (Steve Lorton), 70T; **Larry
Lefever/Grant Heilman Photography:** 4BL; **Margaret
Hensel/Positive Images:** 51 Row 1-1; **Jerry
Howard/Positive Images:** 66TR; **Lee Lockwood/Positive
Images:** 23BR; **Marilyn McAra:** 45TR, 58T, 72T; **Bryan
McCay:** 6TL, 7TR, 26T, 26CR, 26B, 30TL, 30BL, 31TR,
31BL, 31BR, 32TR, 33TR, 33BL, 33BR, 37TR, 37BL,
37BR, 59TL, 59BR, 77BL, 77BC, 77BR, 79BL, 85BL, 88TR,
89CL, 90BL, 91TR, 91CRB, 91BR; **David McDonald/
PhotoGarden:** 17TC, 45TC, 69CR; **Michael McKinley:**
8TL, 9BL (Oehme, van Sweden), 10CL (Robert Chesnut),
11TL, 12T, 13T (Morris & White), 13C (Oehme, van
Sweden), 13B, 14B (David Poot), 15BL (Jack Chandler),
15BR (Oehme, van Sweden), 16BL (Oehme, van Sweden),
16BR (Oehme, van Sweden), 17B (Blue Sky Designs), 18T
(Oehme, van Sweden), 18B (Oehme, van Sweden), 19BC,
20BL (Thomas Church), 21CL (David Benner), 22TL
(Harold Epstein), 22TR (Oehme, van Sweden), 22BL
(Oehme, van Sweden), 40TL, 40BR (John Roberts), 41BR,
44C, 47BL, 51 Row 1-2, 65BR (Oehme, van Sweden),
68CL, 69CL (Thomas Church), 70B, 74C (Jack Chandler),
85TR, 89BL, 89BR (Thomas Church); **Martin
Miller/Positive Images:** 45BC; **Clive Nichols/Jonathan
Baillie:** 49T; **Jerry Pavia:** 73TL; **Susan A. Roth:** 41BL,
89CR; **Eric Salmon:** 27BL, 56BL, 56BR, 57TR, 57BR;
Richard Shiell: 17TR, 45BL; **Guy & Edith Sternberg:**
22BR; **Michael S. Thompson:** 10TR, 11TR, 88BC, 90TL,
91CRT; **judywhite/New Leaf Images:** 8BR

Note to the Readers: Due to differing conditions, tools,
and individual skills, Meredith Corporation assumes no
responsibility for any damages, injuries suffered, or losses
incurred as a result of following the information published
in this book. Before beginning any project, review the
instructions carefully, and if any doubts or questions remain,
consult local experts or authorities. Because codes and
regulations vary greatly, you always should check with
authorities to ensure that your project complies with all
applicable local codes and regulations. Always read and
observe all of the safety precautions provided by
manufacturers of any tools, equipment, or supplies,
and follow all accepted safety procedures.

Ortho® is a trademark of Monsanto Company used
under license.

GETTING THE MOST OUT OF YOUR LANDSCAPE 4

LANDSCAPE SOLUTIONS 10

THINKING ON PAPER 26

HARDSCAPE DESIGN 40

PLANNING FOR SITE PREPARATION 56

PLANTING DESIGN 64

PLANNING FOR EASY MAINTENANCE 84

GETTING THE MOST OUT OF YOUR LANDSCAPE

WHAT YOUR LANDSCAPE CAN DO FOR YOU

Look at your landscape as if for the first time. Envision the possibilities that can be achieved by creating an environment tailored to the needs and wants of you and your family. Try to identify the problems areas. Every problem is an opportunity to create a better landscape.

Let your landscape change your life. This book will show you how to design the space outside your home so it's as attractive and useful as the inside. Instead of looking at landscape design as a subject full of intimidating Latin plant names, think of it as a tool that will make your yard work for you.

Your landscape will serve whatever purpose you desire, and the way you use it will help you divide it subtly into separate zones. Those divisions will allow you to achieve several goals at once. One area may be for entertainment, where friends and family gather; another will offer solitude, escape, and relaxation. You may have a play area for the kids and areas for vegetable and flower gardens as well as for storage.

Landscaping can solve day-to-day problems, too. It can create privacy where there is none, cool overheated, sunlit rooms, and expand a parking area that's now inadequate. It can also get you off the couch and out of doors—yard work and puttering in the garden are rewarding pastimes. And even if yard work is not suited to you (or vice versa), you'll find yourself wanting to spend more time in the pleasant outdoor environment you've created.

INCREASE VALUE

Landscaping adds value to your home. First impressions are everything, and curb appeal will be an immeasurable asset if you put your house on the market. The connection between house and yard will be immediately apparent to buyers, even though they may not be conscious of it. An attractive landscape says, "This home has been well kept and well loved." Conversely, if you're a buyer, don't overlook the potential of a plain house in a nice neighborhood. It will often prove to be a bargain. Adding landscaping that highlights architectural features and hides flaws can turn and uneventful house into a charmer.

But what about the cost? The well-planned landscape can save you money. When you consider all your options, you can choose the one that's best and build it right the first time. Planning the total environment in advance lets you implement as funds permit, without sacrificing the harmony of your design.

THE "SECRETS" OF DESIGN

Good landscaping, however, is more than an enterprise for saving money or adding value to your home. It means more than creating areas of respite and collections of other zones arranged for use. You may hear a landscape designer say, "Let your landscape speak to you," and at first that may sound impractical. But a well-designed landscape is an expression not only of your personality but also the configurations of the land. Where you place the children's play area, for example, or the

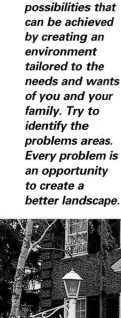

deck or garden pond should be determined not only by convenience, but also by the way they "fit" your yard. So, too, should the edgings and transitions that define them and the materials, contours, and plantings that express your style.

Designing your outdoor space is in many ways not much different from interior design. It is the creation of "living" rooms, with natural or constructed ceilings, walls, and floors, each with its own purpose and decor, each with its own special feeling—that together make a single statement of your personality within the attributes of space.

Don't leave your design instincts inside the back door, but resist the temptation to "get right to it." You'll need a plan, and creating one begins not with a lesson in horticulture,

but with a good working knowledge of the process of design. That's where this book comes in. We'll take you step-by-step through the same procedure designers use to develop lovely and livable landscapes. You'll start first with some general information that will help you explore possibilities and set your goals. Then we'll guide you through the development of your own design, using a chapter-by-chapter evolution of a plan designed for a real landscape.

So go ahead and let your landscape speak. It can tell you things you've never dreamed of. Developing your own plan is a process, and the journey is exciting. Along the way (and when you're done), you may surprise yourself at just how well you've learned to unlock the secrets of design.

The elegance of this pool lies in its quiet simplicity, as well as in the way it rests on the land—as if it belongs there. Such a successful match of man-made form with the shape of the land and a room made of trees doesn't "just happen." It is the product of much thought and careful planning.

DESIGN YOUR DREAMSCAPE

Before: The deck on the southwest corner of our sample site completely lacked privacy and over-shadowed an existing ground-level patio.

Landscape design is a four-part process: research, analysis, conceptualization, and the production of working drawings. It is important to follow the steps in sequence, but it's equally important to realize that your best design will emerge from many revisions. Professional designers always rough out several concepts before choosing the best one. In this book, we'll follow their lead.

The landscape design presented throughout this book is one that was prepared by a landscape architect for a family of four. Refer to the illustrations below as you read through this and the following page. You'll see how their plan evolved (and yours will, too) from a rough conglomeration of ideas, needs, and styles into the finished document you'll use to build your dreamscape.

DESIGN PROGRAM

Before you start even rough sketches for improvements to your yard, equip yourself with information. The more you know about materials that are available, the more you'll be aware of problem solving possibilities. With a knowledge of the methods you can use to create privacy and the areas you need for outdoor living, you'll be confident in setting goals that reflect your personality and family needs. Other tools will help you, too—principles of design, composition, and style. You'll also research your own needs—and dreams. As a result of your efforts in this stage, you'll write a *design program*, which will help you develop the rest of your plans.

SITE ANALYSIS

Conducting a *site analysis* is the next step. You'll examine everything from your interior design to existing outdoor conditions. The way the sun hits your yard, where trees create shade, how the surface water flows, views, and wind patterns—all affect your use of the yard and will impact where you locate play, garden, and pool areas, for example. Understanding existing conditions will help you modify any areas that need improvement and make the most of natural assets.

THE LANDSCAPE DESIGN PROCESS

Mastering the design process will enable you to create a beautiful landscape that meets your needs.

BASE MAP

You'll start by making a Base Map (pages 28-29) to represent your existing property on paper, measuring trees and other features and showing them to scale.

SITE ANALYSIS

Next, you'll conduct a Site Analysis (pages 32-33) to mark problem areas, views, access, and the assets of your landscape. You'll see your yard in a whole new light.

BUBBLE DIAGRAM

Bubble Diagrams (pages 34-35) let you test several schemes for the uses of your yard before you commit to where things go. They will help you examine how each area relates to the others.

CONCEPT DIAGRAM

On your Concept Diagram (pages 36-37)—a sketchy drawing based on your favorite Bubble Diagram— you will begin to refine ideas and make notes about features to include in each area.

CONCEPTUAL DESIGN

Conceptualization is the third phase of design. You'll start by making *bubble diagrams*—quick outlines of areas defined by use—and you'll study how they relate to each other. And you'll change them. The more you explore, the better your design will be. No one will critique your artwork or build a deck from these bubbles; they will be rough and not very specific. For example, on our design (see page 34), we designated an area for entertainment simply as "Gracious/livable."

The next step is a *concept diagram*, and here you'll explore ideas you sketched on your favorite bubble diagram, adding notes about what is needed to make each zone work—this time more specific. Note how the bubble labeled "Gracious/livable" becomes "Entertainment/hardscape" on the concept diagram on page 36.

Although it may seem like a huge leap forward, the *master plan* comes next. You've already laid the foundation for your design. You'll try several versions of each area and fit them together to create your best solution. The designations become more detailed in this stage. The hardscape area in our gracious living zone becomes "Patio" and "Deck" with an overhead arbor connected to the deck (see page 38). Plants are shown by general shapes and labels, not specific names. The master plan will be the foundation for detailed drawings and provide a basis for ballpark cost estimates.

WORKING DRAWINGS

Working drawings direct implementation, specify materials, quantities, sizes, and locations of things you want to add to your landscape. This is where you put in detail—enough to help you build the features yourself or to obtain bids from contractors. You may also find yourself revising your design as the realities of construction become apparent.

You'll make a *layout plan* to guide construction of hardscape, such as patios, walls, and decks. A *grading and drainage plan* will show how you will shape the land for paving and structures, for play or entertaining, and to add interest to the landscape. A *planting plan* shows quantities, spacing, and location of plants. And a *maintenance plan* helps you make caring for your outdoor environment easy.

Even if you plan to hire a designer to prepare working drawings for you, it is important to understand the guiding principles of design outlined in the following chapters. Design the landscape of your dreams. We'll show you how.

Before: Without much front yard planting, our project house lacked distinction.

MASTER PLAN

On your Master Plan (pages 38-39) you'll figure out approximate shapes and locations for planting beds and lawn areas, as well as decks, walkways, parking areas, and other hardscape features.

LAYOUT PLAN

A Layout Plan (pages 54-55) is the next step. You'll trace hardscape elements from your Master Plan, including measurements to scale. And you can still refine your design.

GRADING PLAN

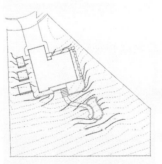

You will show the changes needed to shape your land to accommodate your new design features—either on a conceptual plan that indicates slopes with arrows or with a topography map from which you can prepare a more detailed Grading and Drainage Plan (pages 62-63).

PLANTING PLAN

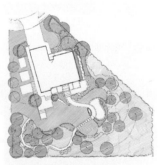

On your Planting Plan (pages 82-83) you'll draw in bed lines that will show the separation between lawn and planting areas. Then you'll decide where trees go and how to fill planting areas with shrubs, ground cover, and seasonal color. Then you can select specific plants by name and make a shopping list.

USE EVERYTHING

When it comes to landscaping, use the whole world as your palette. Take a look around you. Study the contours of your land. Look at other landscapes; watch how trees and shrubs make living rooms. Make note of materials that appeal to you, the kind of walkways you find attractive. Get to know the plants that thrive in your region, and consider amenities such as fountains, pools, and benches. Ask other gardeners about things you like. The research you do now will help you make decisions when you prepare your plans on paper.

Mixed paving materials create an eclectic look, matching the romance of the garden, above. Continuity can be a surprise; the bamboo fence, inset, in front of a bamboo grove repeats the lines and texture of the trees.

NATURAL ELEMENTS

Earth, sky, water, and fire are all elements you may have taken for granted, but each of them can have an effect on your landscape.

The earth itself has a huge influence on design. Landscaping a mountain site, for example, is different from landscaping on the plains. Not only is the terrain of one steep and the other flat, but each has a different soil, and that affects what plants are grown. Rock and stone and boulders are elements of the earth and can contribute to your landscape.

It's important, of course, that you work with the natural characteristics of your site, but that doesn't mean you can't shape it to suit your needs. Grading can yield gently rolling, tranquil hills or level lawns for active children. Steep slopes can be left wooded or neatly planted with ground cover.

Sky is often "overlooked" because it's always there. But the sky can change your landscape. A broad horizon, for example, makes a spectacular view—you may want to remove trees to make the most of such a vista. On the other hand, a heavily wooded site with only glimpses of the sky can create a sheltered feeling. And on a large, flat, treeless site, the sky may seem overwhelming.

Water can work wonders. Still water is a natural mirror; swimming pools are fun. Moving water adds both sound and motion; like liquid music, a waterfall or fountain can make your landscape a world unto itself.

You may never have thought of fire as an aspect of design. But fire is light, and the play of sunlight and shade will influence the location of play and entertainment areas—

An arbor made of trees and limbs found on-site creates structure and preserves a natural look.

The repetition of vertical lines—pale tree trunks—is striking as it ascends the hill. The stair rails highlight the progression of the design.

as well as what and where you plant. Fire and light can lure you into the landscape when you might otherwise stay indoors. A safe fire (in a fire pit or outdoor fireplace) can warm you in chilly weather, and well-planned lighting can bring you out doors after dark.

Wildlife—fish, birds, and other animals—may become a part of the landscape, too, especially if your site is near a woods or you add a garden pool to your plans.

HARDSCAPE AND AMENITIES

Hardscape refers to elements that are constructed—decks, arbors, patios, walkways, steps, driveways, planters, walls, and fences. Hardscape materials offer abundant choices that can influence not only landscape construction but also its beauty and its mood.

Loose gravel or river rock, crushed stone or brick, and decomposed granite give surfaces a soft look. Solid materials such as stone, brick, concrete, asphalt, and wood produce a harder, more definite appearance.

The way you use a material will also have a lot to do with the style it yields. For example, irregular stone appears natural and informal; cut stone lends a formal air. Brick mortared in a slab has a regular, permanent look—quite different from the informality of brick laid in sand. Concrete may be left white or may be tinted or its surface patterned. Asphalt is nearly black when new but fades to a weathered gray. Wood has its own appeal, a natural choice for decks and boardwalks.

Don't limit your look at hardscape to the horizontal. All of these materials may be used vertically, as well. You may want to build a wall, an arbor, or a shed for utility storage. Metal has a place in the landscape, too, in trellises and arbors, gates and fences, and in railings and artwork. Rope and chain make rails or vine supports. Fabric forms umbrellas, blinds, cushions, and awnings—even tents.

Then there are amenities—a garden pond or fountain, a stream with waterfalls, objects such as benches and sculpture, architectural relics, swings, wind chimes, and items that express your personal style.

PLANTING

Plants, of course, are integral to all landscape styles. Trees, shrubs, ground covers, vines, lawns, perennials, and annuals make your choices nearly endless. Plants add color and texture to the landscape and can establish the lines that define your style—in bedlines that curve across your yard or in grids that grow in geometric configurations. Plants can add privacy, frame entrances or views, and make structures look at home. Plants add scale, too. A two-story home, for example, may dwarf a person standing beside it, but add a tree or other element of intermediate height, and the proportions feel more human.

When you're planning for plants, add to your research some knowledge of your climate and the conditions in your yard. Every site has limitations, and yours is no exception, but if you know them, you will choose plants that will thrive in your landscape. Limitations, after all, are only opportunities for design.

Don't be afraid to combine materials. Old brick makes an excellent companion for pea gravel. Wood and stone are natural partners.

You'll find further information on materials and the other elements of design as you read through the following pages. But be sure you read the entire book before you start making plans on paper. Landscape design, although sequential, is also cyclical. It's a process of revision and refinement; the more you know about each aspect and its relationship to all the others, the more exciting the process will be and the better your design.

Brick, tile, and casual, open furnishings combine with background plants to bring a sense of warmth and comfort to this entertainment area.

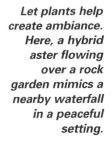

Let plants help create ambiance. Here, a hybrid aster flowing over a rock garden mimics a nearby waterfall in a peaceful setting.

Taming a slope can take an artistic turn. These treated lumber steps curve invitingly up the landscape; had they climbed straight up, they would have seemed daunting on this hillside.

The wooden front of this utility structure not only conceals storage, it becomes the background for a garden focal point. Spaces between the planks allow air to circulate and encourage a vine to weave its way upward.

Locate family parking areas along the kitchen side of the house for easy grocery-toting. When calculating parking area, allow a 9 by 20 foot space for each car. That's the size of most parking lot spaces.

Your landscape can meet specific needs just as rooms in your house do. A spot for firewood is an inexpensive yet valuable asset, and it's easy to add. Building this storage area against an existing wall cuts construction costs and keeps the wood stacked neatly. Always locate storage areas close to areas they serve— in this case, the door nearest the fireplace.

Garbage cans and yard tools can be close at hand without necessarily spoiling your view. Screen them out by planting evergreen shrubs, erecting wooden fences or trellises, or extending walls to form hidden utility areas. This stone wall and wooden gate blends in handsomely with the rest of the design. It's also dog proof.

LANDSCAPE SOLUTIONS

LANDSCAPES THAT MAKE YOUR LIFE EASIER

Form follows function is the slogan of good design. Although aesthetics are important in design development, your landscape must be practical as well as pretty. For example, guests may find your front-door walkway attractive, but if it's too narrow for walking side by side, they may choose to enter through your garage instead. Likewise, a quiet retreat that lacks seating won't get much use. On the other hand, if you locate your outdoor dining area just outside your kitchen door—and make it comfortable—it may prove to be the most popular spot of your home.

DESIGN FOR EASE

Let your needs dictate your plans. Then meet those needs with solutions that are both practical and attractive. Adequate, easy parking, for example, is a common goal. But don't stop there; parking can be pretty, too. Surround the turnaround you want with a retaining wall, add in fill soil behind it, and plant weeping shrubs that will billow over the top.

Or, stain the concrete to a warm brown to minimize its intrusion in the landscape. Pave a level parking surface with decorative gravel or crushed stone instead of an impermeable material—a solution that blends parking with the landscape and may solve drainage problems, too. Then with a few small, ornamental trees (that may be all that's needed), separate your new parking area from the entry to your home.

Begin looking at your landscape for all the everyday problems you've never had the time to solve. They are opportunities for design. For example, are you constantly moving the car to get the lawn mower out? Consider a storage shed to keep the practical things in life where you can find them when you need

Small changes in your lawn design can save you time maintaining it. Mow curbs, like this one made of brick, keep grass and planting beds separate. Their level surface makes close cuts possible and reduces the need for edgers or string trimmers.

them (dress it up with trellises and vines). A pathway worn in the lawn means there probably should have been a gravel walk or other hardscape path there in the first place.

Now is the time to start thinking about particular zones you want to include in your landscape—that open space for the kids to play, the sunny spot for raising vegetables, the place for entertaining friends and family. You don't need to make a list now—that can come later. But now's the time to look at the potential of your landscape with an eye toward making life easier.

Underground sprinkler systems let you control the amount of water your lawn receives. Instead of watering a little every day, you can water less frequently—but thoroughly. This promotes deep root growth, which makes grass more tolerant of drought.

SMART YARDS

Spend more time enjoying your landscape and less time maintaining it. Plan ahead. Examine your chore time and let design solutions reduce it in the future. For example, stop trying to grow grass where it doesn't want to grow. Make plans to fill that bare spot with a shrub-and-ground-cover bed or replace it with paving. Study plants so you will choose the right one for the right place—you won't have to coax it to grow or prune it constantly to fit its allotted space. Any effort you expend now in research will pay off in time saved later.

OUTDOOR COMFORT

Outdoor comfort should be a priority when you design the exterior of your home. But face it—the great outdoors can sometimes be too hot, too cold, too windy, too wet, and too full of tiny flying things that bite. Don't let nature chase you indoors. There is a bag of design tricks you can employ to make your outdoor living areas comfortable and inviting.

SUN AND SHADE

Watch how the sun crosses your landscape. Plan to protect western exposures in hot climates and northern exposures in regions that are cold. If your yard will host the neighborhood touch-football league or small-fry soccer, orient the playing fields on a north-south axis to keep the sun out of the contestants' eyes.

Shade can have both a positive and negative impact on the livability of your landscape. It's cool and inviting, but if there's too much of it, it can seem dim and dreary. Mosquitoes seem to prefer shady spots over open areas, too.

Dappled shade will give you the best of both worlds. Honey locust is a classic tree for dappled shade. Its open leaves and branches let in just the right amount of sunlight. Locate shade trees so they cast a shadow on favorite areas when the sun is directly overhead. Trees planted to the east of your home will reduce the heat of morning sun; trees along the west will cool it in the afternoon. Deciduous species (they lose their leaves during dormancy) will give you summer shade, but when they're leafless, they will let in the warming winter rays. Balance shade with sunny zones for interest.

A low hedge is all that's needed to separate this patio from the rest of the yard, and the fencing adds privacy to this cozy and comfortable sitting area.

Evergreen shrubs form a dense hedge that shields this intimate garden from winds that sweep in from the hillside. The hedges also provide a neutral background for perennial beds and make the flowers more noticeable.

BUFFER PLANTING

Plants can block harsh winds and reduce noise and nighttime glare. Tall, sturdy evergreens along the northwestern edge of your property can knock down bitter winds. Strategically planted trees can cut off the glare of headlights shining into windows at night. Combine plants with solid walls for sound barriers. They do double duty— walls block sound and foliage absorbs it.

CIRCULATE THE AIR AND WATER

Increase the air circulation across your yard and eliminate stagnant water and you'll do more to reduce the biting insect population than any bug zapper. Consider adding pergolas so you can mount exterior ceiling fans to do the bug shooing for you. Latticework with vines offers privacy without blocking breezes.

Moving water in your water feature will also reduce mosquito breeding. Install a submersible pump; they're sold in kits and are the easiest way to keep the water moving. Remove anything that collects rainwater from your yard; don't have a bird bath unless you're committed to tossing out the water in the basin every few days and replacing it with fresh water. Finally, consider screening a section of your deck or patio. You'll enjoy fresh air without the bugs.

Think about other comfort factors, such as privacy, accessibility, and sitting places, so your design will make the most of your yard.

Low-voltage lights can transform your landscape. They enhance views from within your house and give outdoor spots an after-hours appeal. Uplighting trees highlights their form. Downlighting from within creates a glow that illuminates pathways and steps.

Paving doesn't have to mean poured concrete. Cut stones set in a sand bed can turn a shady spot into your favorite sitting area. Tucked along the edge of the property, this patio is shielded from view by a privacy fence. Furniture and flowers make this easy design solution an inviting retreat.

Secret of Splash
Adding a water feature is a favorite designer trick for masking noise. The pleasant sound of falling water is a wonder worker. However, don't go overboard, or conversations will turn into shouting matches. Just a little water movement can make a delightful difference.

PRIVACY

Planting for privacy doesn't have to mean formal, clipped hedges. Flowering trees and shrubs can add an air of intimacy and color to a seating-area composition. For screens, combine deciduous plants with fences or with evergreen plants. You'll have both seasonal interest and year-round structure.

Your home interior has shared spaces and private spaces, and so should your landscape. Landscape architects frequently rank establishing privacy as a top priority in landscaping projects. That's because they know you're more likely to use your yard if you don't feel you're on display.

Plan for privacy, and start plants growing where you need them right away. Building fences or walls early on makes it easier to move on to other projects, such as flower beds, without incurring construction damage at a later date. Then you can plant around those structures and soften the raw look of new construction.

As you evaluate your privacy needs, consider all possible solutions. Fencing will fix some situations, but plants will work best in others. A fence or hedge along your property line is one solution, but it may not be the best. Carefully placed natural buffers (trees or shrubs) can solve two dilemmas at once. They can screen individual personal areas of your yard and can give them definition at the same time. You can shape your separate garden spaces and won't be left feeling that what you've built is a stockade.

Don't limit your considerations of privacy to merely blocking neighbors' views. Dividing your landscape into outdoor rooms means that you will want to establish a hierarchy of privacy within your landscape similar to your home interior. Just as your bedroom is more private than your living room, your garden will have spaces that are intimate and spaces that are shared.

PLANTING FOR PRIVACY

Plants, depending on your selection, can give you either seasonal or year-round privacy. If it's unbroken privacy you need, educate yourself about evergreens. In the plant world, they do the best job of providing continuous screening. Because evergreens, such as holly and conifers, shed and replace their foliage a little at a time instead of losing them all at once in autumn, they retain plenty of view-blocking greenery even in winter. Add a knowledge of which plants are evergreen and which are deciduous to your research goals.

Vines, also, are great for adding privacy. Because they grow up and over (trellises and walls, for example), vines are like living cloaks. Plant a fast-growing annual or tropical vine together with a slower-growing species. You'll get a quick screen that in time will be replaced with one that is permanent.

Total privacy is not always needed, of course. You can achieve degrees of privacy by mixing deciduous plants in with evergreens. Or, omit the evergreens entirely.

Sometimes the form of a plant is enough to establish a sense of separation between you and other spaces. For example, the trunks and limbs of river birch or aspen provide a feeling of enclosure even when their leaves drop for winter.

Enclosing an area creates a courtyard effect. As views looking out (and upward) are blocked, attention is directed inward, making the most of small focal points such as this sculpture.

DESIGN TIP

Landscaping can solve privacy problems inside your house, too. Blinds and drapes that you never open are a sure sign you need to add exterior screening.

Privacy need not be total to be effective. Tree-form shrubs add a degree of separation to this sitting area without completely obscuring the views.

STAGGERED PLANTING

Set buffer plants along a zigzag pattern instead of in straight rows. You'll get a denser screen more quickly without the expense of a double row of plants.

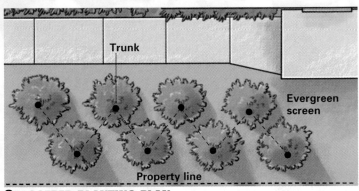

STAGGERED PLANTING PLAN

FENCING

Your fence selection should also relate to your privacy needs. Tall, wooden fences and solid walls offer the most immediate forms of total privacy. You may need tall fences to screen a courtyard, but shorter fencing will be more appropriate for other areas. For example, in the front yard—usually the most public section of the landscape—waist-high picket fences work well. They define the space but allow you to chat with neighbors. Open metal fencing can likewise add a decorative touch without completely blocking all views.

Though fences provide quick solutions, they don't grow. But plants do. Combine the two to meet both long-and short-term needs. Wire fencing, though unattractive, will immediately keep children and pets from straying; shrubs, vines, and trees will grow to make them pretty.

SECURITY

Privacy and security are often at odds with one another. A solid fence will make your garden private, but a thief may roam about undetected. Combine solid and see-through fencing for privacy that doesn't sacrifice security. Lights triggered by motion-sensors will also intimidate intruders.

The right plant in the right place also enhances security. Correctly selected foundation shrubs will stay below window height with a minimum of pruning. Conversely, plants whose mature height outgrows their allotted space can shield break-ins from view. Consider adding thorny or sharp-leafed shrubs beneath first-floor windows. Avoid planting low-limbed trees near your home; they can serve as natural ladders to the upper floors.

Lattice panels can be used as baffles to control views and still allow easy access. This side-door entry maintains comfortable access while protecting the rear yard from view.

This vine-covered lattice screen turns an air conditioner into a thing of beauty and lets the air circulate around it. Lattice is also excellent for concealing utility areas and great for creating private outdoor garden rooms or screening views from the outside of your home.

OUTDOOR LIVING

Make the most of your property—continue the activities of the indoors into the outdoors. Don't limit your landscape to a mere collection of plants and other decorations. Your landscape plan can offer you a place for play, a relaxation area, an exercise zone and fun spots for gathering with friends and family. Think about what you and your family would like to do outside and plan your space to meet these needs. In design circles this step is known as user analysis, and it's just one tool that you can use to tailor the outdoors to better meet your needs. You may find suggestions in the photos on this page. Keep these ideas in mind when you compile a wish list later in the process.

VIEWS AND TRANSITIONS

Consider also the relationship you will be creating between interior and exterior spaces. Design your landscape so that the view through interior windows looks out on garden space instead of dull or unattractive sights. (Pleasant views will also mean you'll keep the curtains open, letting in more natural light.)

Turn your backyard into a vacation-like escape by adding places for relaxing and entertaining—even exercise. This pool deck provides plenty of living area for an active family, making it a favorite gathering spot throughout the year.

Let your landscape serve your family. Study your yard and dedicate a portion of it to your children's play. Mulch reduces injuries from falling and keeps maintenance to a minimum. Paved walkways are great for riding toys. It's a good idea to add seating nearby for adults.

Simple and uncluttered designs will make the most of natural vistas and help celebrate exterior views. Minimal planting, a little shade, comfortable seating, and easy access will lure you out into the landscape to admire the view.

The garden can be your link with nature, even if you're a city dweller. Plant flowers to attract winged creatures, and set some chairs outside to enjoy your own little oasis.

Interior views that look out on the landscape will also keep the walls from closing in around you, especially in a smaller home.

That small house or a confining room can seem bigger when the outdoor space is properly designed. Stepping out onto a generous patio "expands" the floor space inside. Consider replacing a narrow stoop with a deck. (You may be able to build the deck right over the stoop without removing it.) If you don't have the space or budget to build an area large enough to throw a party, a landing big enough for a bench and a few flowers will do nicely, making the transition from indoors less abrupt. It also provides a pleasant spot for a cup of coffee on a pretty morning (and a good place for muddy boots and wet umbrellas).

WHICH WAY DOES THE TRAFFIC GO?

You may find that changes to the interior of your house will improve its indoor/outdoor connection. Sketch the floor plan of your house and label each room. Show the location of doors and windows. Examine the flow of family traffic and how people move into and out of your house. Mark these routes with arrows. Then rearrange the furniture to open views and paths to the outdoors or consider converting existing windows to French doors.

You'll spend a lot more time in your yard if you furnish areas with features that turn them into destinations. Consider what you'd like to do in your landscape and design outdoor living areas to accommodate your needs. You can add something as elaborate as the spa (left), or as simple as a comfortable spot to sit and have a snack (above). Although most people like to engage in some type of activity, they will also look for places to sit, so you'll probably rarely use an area that is for standing only.

Color in the landscape is useful for capturing attention and helps tie a landscape together. The hue of these 'Autumn Joy' sedum blossoms is echoed in the tint of the ornamental grasses and in background flower beds.

Texture is an often overlooked element of design, but it can add depth to a composition. Large leaves bring coarse textures to the landscape; many small leaves contribute fine texture. Make your design even more interesting by layering contrasting textures.

Lines affect emotions. This zigzag bench gives a sense of movement and activity to the composition. Smoothly flowing lines can bring natural and peaceful qualities.

BEAUTIFUL SPACE

In nature, beautiful space just happens. But when you add a house and hardscape, the native beauty changes. With a knowledge of design elements (the building blocks) and principles (the methods for manipulating them), you'll be able to create space that unifies your needs with natural beauty.

BUILDING BLOCKS FOR DESIGN

Color, texture, line, and form are the four main elements of design.

COLOR is the easiest element to identify but can be the hardest one to use. Because color expresses emotion, it's easy to use too much. The predominant color in your landscape will, of course, be green, and shades of green and hardscape will act as the background in most of your design. Carefully plan your placement of accent color—the fun stuff— against this background so the accents don't get lost or misapplied.

For example, brightly blooming zinnias will accent an ivied wall or a gated garden view. They will not stand out with others in a bed, and planted at the base of a telephone pole, they call attention to an unattractive feature.

Color impact varies also with its quantity. Dense patches command your view; thin lines are distracting. Limiting colors to a few or sprinkling a single color throughout a mixture of hues creates a unified composition and avoids competing accents.

TEXTURE refers to tactile qualities. Fine-textured plants have many small leaflets, needles, or twigs. Coarse-textured plants have fewer and broader leaves. Pea gravel produces fine-textured surfaces; stones are considered coarse. Fine and coarse textures juxtaposed throughout the landscape add contrasting interest. A smooth, gray stone set in a bed of narrow-leaved mondo grass (*Ophiopogon japonica*) creates a pleasing textural accent in a composition whose colors are unremarkable. Use textural contrasts, like their color counterparts, sparingly for best results.

LINE describes visual paths in a composition. Tree trunks contribute vertical lines. Level ground establishes the horizontal. Lines can be curved (separating sinuous planting beds from paving) or straight (setting off angular walkways from the lawn). You don't have to limit your design to only one type, but when you combine types, let one kind dominate. For example, a landscape with curved bedlines may successfully include a square patio, but the curved bedlines are dominant to the straight lines and right angles.

FORM, of course, refers to shape. The form of a plant—upright, pendulous, pyramidal, or spreading—describes its growth habit, and like the other elements, form lends itself to complement and contrast. For example, plants with pendulous forms, such as weeping willow (*Salix babylonica*) often look wonderful with garden ponds. The vertical branches contrast with the horizontal plane of water.

COMPOSING WITH PRINCIPLES

Though many parts make up the whole, your design will be more successful if you view it (and design it with the following principles), not as a collection of single elements, but as a harmonious composition.

UNITY ties things together, and repetition, rhythm, and sequence are the tools you'll use to create it. Repeating an element—color, texture, line, or form—is an easy way to give a scene a unifying theme. The same brick paving in both a patio and a path unites the hardscape with repeated color and shape. Repetition can be rhythmic or random. Rhythmic patterns are regular and create a sense of expectation—finials spaced evenly on fence post tops, for example. A random scattering of white blossoms throughout your flower beds unifies them informally. Sequence conveys movement from one stage to another. Your landscape style may begin with formal design near the house and become less formal at the end of your yard. Unity is maintained by the gradual progression of styles.

BALANCE. You'll recognize balance in a landscape because it makes things look and feel comfortable. Balance can be symmetrical (straight lines, right angles, and mirror-image arrangements) or asymmetrical (curved lines, irregular shapes, and casual composition). If it's symmetry you want (it's almost always formal), repeat an element in even-numbered groupings. For asymmetrical design, plan odd-numbered groupings and use dissimilar items for balance. For example, a single, large tree can balance a bed of numerous small shrubs.

ACCENT is the spice of design. Any element can become an accent if it contrasts with its surroundings. Accents may be as small as a blossom or as large as a bright red foot bridge. But remember to place them where you want to draw attention (they are often best against a neutral background). The front door is a good place to start. So is the far end of a walkway; your guests will follow it to see what's there. Think in terms of multiple accents—contrasts of both color and texture, for example. They will add interest to your landscape. Sprinkle them with care so they won't compete or contribute to a case of scenic overload.

The rich texture of the herringbone-patterned brick, the repetition of white blossoms, and the straight-lined paths and hedges work together to make this garden a lovely formal composition.

The pyramidal form of a conifer acts as a terminus for the line of the curving walk. Repetition of flower colors unifies the large scene.
The arching form of an arbor (inset) creates a window into this garden that is echoed by another arbor at the opposite end.

A brilliant stained-glass window does double duty, serving both as an interior feature and as an exterior focal point for this roof garden. Lush, container-grown plants are arranged to frame the window and give the area an intimate mood. Using minimal color in the planting plays up the accent qualities of the window.

STYLE

Style is the presentation of design. Landscape design may assume all sorts of different styles but can be broadly categorized as either formal or informal. Examine landscapes that appeal to you and try to distinguish among styles so you'll know what you like. Different styles may be appropriate for different areas of your landscape. For example, you may choose a formal style for your front yard and an informal style for the back yard.

The pattern formed by marigolds bordering similar shaped beds gives this ornamental vegetable garden a decidedly formal air.

FORMAL DESIGN

Formal designs use visual cues to create a sense of expectation, much in the same way the sight of a tuxedo might make you think of an elegant event. In landscape design, symmetry (see page 19) is one such cue, and matched pairs are one way of establishing symmetry.

Pairs instantly add a formal touch. A pair of urns, for example, will lend a stately air to your front steps. A pair of plants frames whatever is beyond it.

Two of the same item become an instantly recognizable unit, even if the items are not placed side by side. Even-numbered groupings create this same effect. The pattern of expectation is regular, orderly, and at rest. Geometric shapes—clearly defined circles, squares, rectangles, singly or in combinations—also establish formality. To create formality in your own plan, consider introducing these shapes in arches, paving patterns, fences, and bed designs.

INFORMAL DESIGN

Informal design strives for the unexpected and creates a casual yet balanced mood. Odd-numbered groupings—a cluster of three ornamental shrubs growing in a ground cover bed—keep the design dynamic. Consider adding triangles to your design. Three trees planted at different points on an invisible triangle along a walkway provide canopies without the formality of even-numbered rows. This trick works for any odd-numbered plant groupings as well, and repetition of elements in informal design schemes need not follow a regular pattern.

COMPLEMENTS, CONTRASTS, AND COMBINATIONS

The architecture of a home often influences landscape style. An imposing federalist house

A study in balanced contrast: Clipped hedges, matching French planter boxes, and an Italianate pool make the perfect formal frame for this natural view of Napa Valley, California.

Alternating squares of ground cover and striking vertical columns give this Chicago garden formality with a modern twist.

with stately columns may be complemented by a formal landscape design. A quaint cottage may be the perfect setting for curving paths bordered by informally mixed plantings. However, the style of the house does not have to dictate what will happen in the landscape. A contrasting style in the grounds will soften the dominant presence of the architecture— but the landscape design must be clearly formal or informal. Don't settle for something in between: The resulting ambiguity will look like a mistake.

That's not to say that formal and informal designs cannot contain their opposites. There's nothing quite like rounding a bend to discover a tidy pocket of formality growing neatly inside a naturalistic landscape. Mixed styles require planning. For example, formal walkways combined with informal beds are charming. The trick to succeeding with any cross of styles is to know what you're after. Study photographs of gardens that appeal to you to see what style is just right. Then you can apply the elements and principles of design in the style you find appropriate.

The neat lines of picket fence contrast with a profuse and informal planting of flowers in this New England cottage garden. Its carefree look is supported by structural elements.

A blanket of moss succeeds in growing where grass wouldn't in this mid-Atlantic landscape. The owner removed remaining spots of lawn and let moss fill the area with velvety texture, enhancing the already naturalistic style.

SENSE OF PLACE

Geographic regions have a great influence on style. Using materials indigenous to your region helps your landscape fit in its surroundings. Borrowing styles from other areas can add flavor to your design, but unless your goal is to replicate a foreign environment, take care to preserve a local sense of place. Your design will seem at home in its site, rather than imposed upon it.

The bold form of an agave contrasts with smooth walls tinted in bright desert colors, adding a southwestern flavor to a garden whose style reflects its geographic location.

Informal doesn't mean unplanned. Black-eyed Susans framing a stone walk provide striking color and form in this expression of a Midwestern prairie.

PLANTING FOR THE SEASONS

Summer-blooming perennials are a great way to color hot-weather retreats. 'Moonbeam' coreopsis and blazing star thrive in the sun, as do garden phlox, garlic chives, and coneflowers. Pots of heat-tolerant annuals will put on seasonal displays, too.

It wouldn't be spring without a flush of flowers. Candy-colored azaleas and rhododendrons are traditional favorites for welcoming the season. Drifts of like colors bring the best show. Plan to include plants that are showy in other seasons; they'll carry on when spring blossoms are just a memory.

Autumn is a wonderful time to be out-of-doors, so don't forget to add seasonal interest that carries into fall. Maple leaves turn bright colors, 'Autumn joy' sedum bears rusty blooms, and plumes top ornamental grasses. Mums, Russian sage, and fall-blooming asters come into their own.

Winter is the time to admire the lines and forms in your garden. Plump evergreen shrubs and feathery conifers take on a new grace when the rest of the garden is dormant. Bare branches of sycamore, river birch, and Japanese maple add sculpture to cold-weather scenes.

Each season brings its own distinct beauty to the landscape. With a little advance planning on your part, you can bring the flow of seasonal display into your own design.

Flowers put on the most obvious seasonal show. Spring is just the beginning; summer and fall boast blossoms, too. Winter will keep color in your garden in warmer climates and form and structure where it's cold.

Fruits are natural decorations. Many berries ripen in fall and winter, and their clusters brighten snowy scenes. Seed pods and other fruit add interest throughout the seasons.

Don't forget the leaves—foliage color has a huge impact on landscape design. Variegated foliage (with more than one color on each leaf) ranges across the spectrum. You'll find leaves and needles from white to yellow to nearly blue and endless shades in between.

Form and texture come into their own when plants are dormant. Winter landscape is like a black-and-white photo; shapes and tactile qualities dominate. Bark, trunks, and branches take on sculptural qualities, especially when coated with ice or snow.

Try combining evergreen and deciduous plants. The dark foliage and pleasing shapes of evergreens provides the perfect foil for color during warm seasons and shows off the form of leafless plants in winter. Don't keep the evergreens always in the background. Plan them for year-round beauty.

INSTANT BEAUTY

River birch is a fast-growing tree that can provide shade and vertical definition while you wait for slower-growing hardwoods. Red maple is also quick for shade (avoid the weaker-wooded silver maple). Many small ornamental trees such as cherries and crape myrtles can make a big difference in just a few growing seasons.

Vines and climbing roses can dress up a landscape in a hurry. Give roses at least six full hours of sun each day and fertilize regularly. Start vines right away to add texture and color to your landscape. Most vines can grow at double or triple the rate of other woody plants, giving gardens quick appeal while new trees and shrubs are getting started.

It doesn't take years and years to grow flowers. Prepare planting beds with soil rich in organic matter and add sand if your drainage is poor. Then you're ready to plant perennials in your garden. In just one season, you can have a blanket of blossoms. Remember to plan ahead for color during different seasons.

PLANTING FOR RAPID EFFECT

It's wonderful to have an old growth stand of timber along a landscape border, but trees take years to mature. Meanwhile, little saplings are not attractive.

It is possible, however, to get things growing and still plant for the future. For example, plant paper birches in front of beeches on a border. The bark of the birches will be immediately beautiful and provide the right companionship for the slower growing beeches. You'll have focal points for now and for the future.

Or plant ornamental shrubs in front of a grove of saplings. The shrubs will attract your attention until the trees claim their place.

Planting big trees is another way to give your landscape a new look right away. Tree spades can dig large specimens that have been root-pruned in advance. It's best to plant trees in fall after plants have stopped actively growing and before the ground freezes. Feeder roots have time to get established before the spring growing season begins. Big trees can cost a lot, as you pay for the size of the plant and equipment and labor to move it. Purchase a one-year guarantee if possible. If you can't afford big trees, don't worry. Plant a small one—time and patience will prove that all trees of the same species end up approximately the same size at maturity, regardless of their size upon planting.

BRAINSTORMING YOUR DESIGN PROGRAM

An elegant entry may be tops on your wish list. Colorful plantings in neatly bordered beds, attractive paving, and wide steps make this entryway impressive.

Combine new paving and planting to provide a place for outdoor entertaining or a family meal.

Now it's time to do some wishful thinking—to transform the results of all your research and ideas into the steps that will make the landscape work for you.

You'll need to make several lists, first a wish list—the things you've always wanted in your landscape—then a needs list—those items you really need. Then you'll combine them, refine them, and draw up your design program.

WISH LIST

Jot down things you've always wanted, regardless of budget concerns. It's important to let your imagination run wild at this point. (The time for realism will come later.) Make

your notes quickly to allow your ideas to flow. Minimal descriptions will do the job: "swimming pool with waterfall," for example. List at least 10 to 15 items, including major elements of style and things you want for decoration. When you're finished, rank them in the order of their importance.

Ask family members to produce their own dream lists and to rank them also. Then combine all the lists into a master wish list. There will now be several wishes in each priority, reflecting what each person wants. Leave them unranked within the priorities or create rankings within each level.

WHAT DO YOU NEED?

Now make a second list. This will be your needs list. For example, perhaps you need more guest parking. Maybe you need to make your home look more welcoming. Don't forget to consider indoor needs, too. You may need additional privacy at one window or more natural light coming in another. Rank your needs as you did your wishes. Gather needs lists from your family into a master needs list.

Next, compare the two. Are any of your needs and dreams similar? Your wish list may contain a stone patio, and that will meet the need you listed for "entertainment area." Match as many items on the two lists as possible and put stars by them.

Now look at what's left on the two lists (items that don't have stars). There are probably plenty of needs, say, garbage can storage, that aren't included on your wish list,

Turn a worn trail through planting beds into a garden path by setting stones and planting herbs, ground cover, and bulbs to grow between them.

and vice versa. Are there any wishes you would sacrifice in order to meet needs? Can low-ranking needs be omitted?

If there's something you really want that doesn't meet a specific need, keep that idea as a priority anyway. You can try to find a way to make it fit into your landscape, or you can omit it later. Review the lists and eliminate those things everyone agrees are less important. Then combine the surviving wishes and needs and rank them by consensus. The result is your design program, which will be the foundation for your budget decisions and will guide you through several steps when you put your plans on paper.

REALITY CHECK

Take a hard look at your design program. Chances are, your desires exceed your budget, but there may be ways to modify your dreams.

Though you can't obtain accurate cost estimates until you produce a master plan, look for money-saving ideas now. Take "swimming pool with waterfall," for example. Do you want a place to swim or do you really want a waterfall? If you can't have both, can you settle for one? Or for smaller versions of either? Small waterfalls can be affordable. So can smaller pools. If any such major installation is beyond your budget right now, go ahead and plan its future location. You may be able to build it in the future.

Use your design program as a guide— you probably won't actually implement every item. The purpose of writing a program is not to cram in everything you've ever wanted, but to identify those items so you can choose what you really want and how they relate to your budget and the rest of the landscape. Don't build a waterfall merely because you've always wanted one. Build it with design sense. It should serve as a focal point, mask annoying sounds, or add movement to a static area.

Understanding how each element serves your design may reveal uses or locations you've never thought of and will make their incorporation more effective. Some things won't be appropriate to your site. Others will be perfect. Be objective. Refer to your design program when you need help making decisions and keep it handy for sketching conceptual designs. You've gone through a lot of thoughtful work already, and you'll find it paying off when you begin to compose your landscape plan.

DESIGN PROGRAM

The design program below corresponds to the sample plans used throughout this book. It will give you an idea of how yours might look.

- ■ Attractive entry area
- ■ Vegetable gardening
- ■ Outdoor entertainment area for family and friends
- ■ Quiet spot for relaxation
- ■ Wildlife feeding station
- ■ Access to woods
- ■ Open lawn area for children to play
- ■ Better circulation from front yard to back
- ■ Less lawn to mow
- ■ Colorful plantings
- ■ Privacy from neighbor

Thinking on paper puts you in the position of looking at your property from a bird's-eye view. Instead of getting bogged down with details, you can play with ideas. At this stage of your project, it is more important to examine the relationships between areas of your yard than it is to pick flower colors—that can come later. From the vantage point a drawing offers, you can see how different zones of your yard work together, how they fail to work, and what you can do to make them work. Skipping this step means you begin planning solutions before you've thoroughly analyzed your site and considered how you want to use it.

THINKING ON PAPER

GETTING STARTED

Homes are built from detailed house plans. A successful landscape is just as dependent on a carefully executed, written landscape plan.

What you've learned so far has already gotten you started in the landscape design process. Now for the fun part: You're going to learn how to "think on paper." You'll start making your own plan by tracing a base map of your property. Then you'll plan the use of your existing spaces by producing overlay drawings known as bubble diagrams. Next, you'll expand your favorite bubble diagram to create a concept diagram, and that will form the basis for your master plan.

Remember that revision is a natural part of the design process. Capturing your ideas on paper makes it easy to consider all the possibilities while you can still easily change your mind. If you aren't an accomplished artist, don't worry; there's no need to produce a pretty plan. Scribble, erase, and cross things out as much as you like. Nothing is set in stone; that's why you design on paper before you start setting the stones!

Until you can view your site and its major features, such as your house and driveway, it is impossible to decide what should go where and how much room you have to work with. To find this information, you'll begin by making a base map that accurately represents your property. You can use the plot plan that you received in the closing documents when you bought your home, but you'll need to enlarge it (see page 29).

Plot plans are normally small drawings that fit on a regular-sized sheet of paper. They are drawn to scale, meaning that an inch equals a certain number of feet. The scale of the plan tells you how to read its dimensions. For example, the notation 1" = 10' means that every inch on your plan represents 10 feet in "real life." Your plan may be drawn at 20 scale (1" = 20'), 30 scale, etc. The scale you are working with will be noted on the plan.

The word "scale" also refers to a special kind of ruler called an engineer's scale. Learning how to use an engineer's scale will allow you to accurately represent landscape features on paper. You'll also be able to determine how many plants will fit in a certain area of your yard. And, because you'll have a good idea of quantities needed, you can figure out how much your landscape will cost before you buy the first plant.

You'll also be able to determine the workability of other features you are considering, such as patios, swimming pools, and walkways—and alter your plan as needed.

READING AN ENGINEER'S SCALE

The easiest way to read your plan dimensions accurately is with an engineer's scale. This is a triangular ruler that has inches divided into different increments, each representing a different length. For example, on the side of the scale that is marked 10, an inch is divided into 10 equal parts. Each part is equivalent to 1 foot. Half an inch equals 5 feet, 2 inches equal 20 feet, and so on. Use this side if your drawing is labeled 1" = 10'. Use other sides of the ruler to measure plans drawn at other scales.

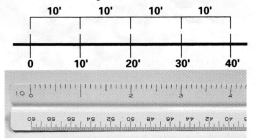

SCALE: 1" = 10'

PLANNING TOOLS

These can be found at an art supply store.

- Engineer's scale
- Roll of tracing paper
- 2 circle templates, ranging from ¼" to 3½" in diameter
- Thick and thin black felt-tipped pens

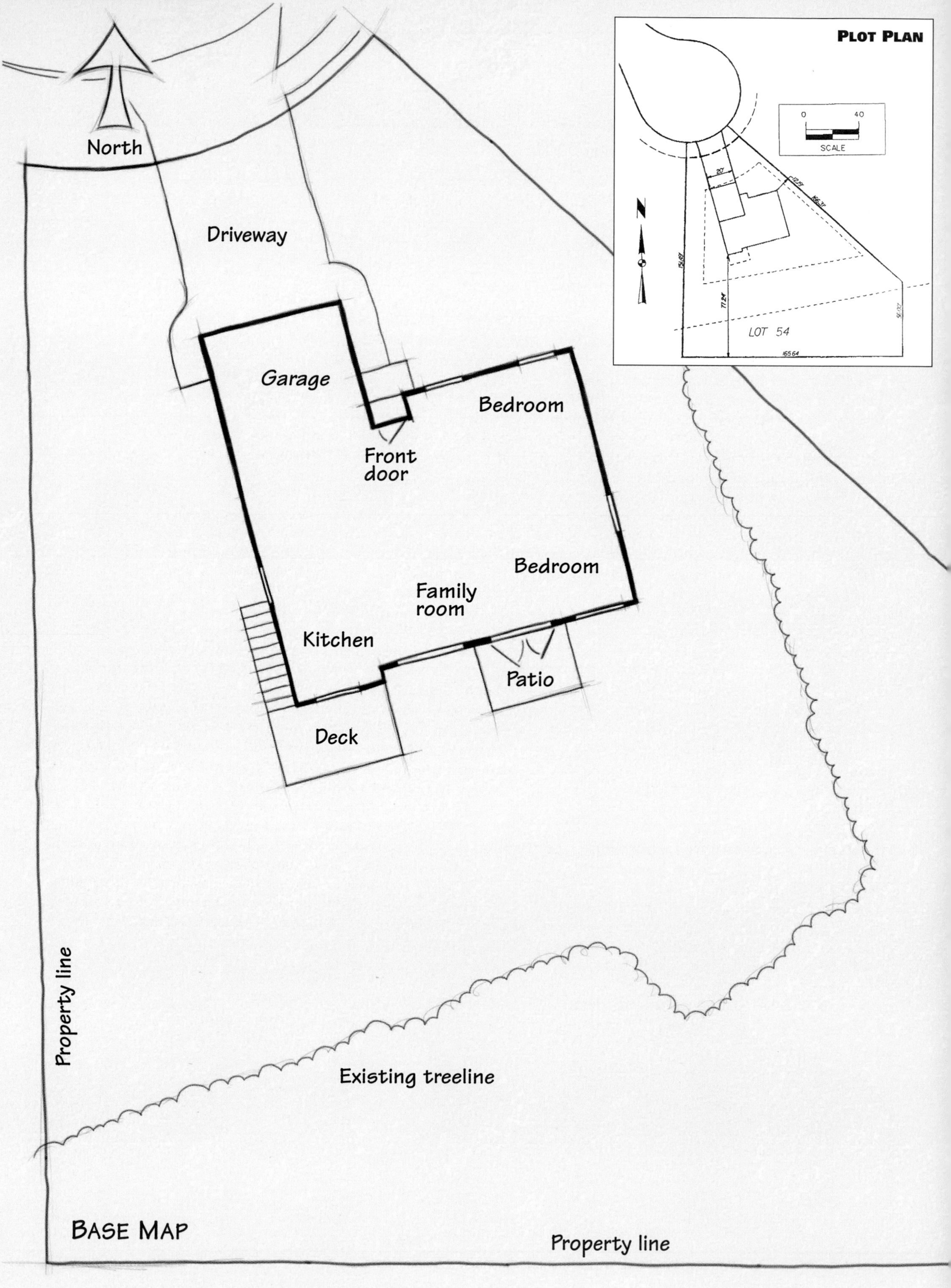

North

Driveway

Garage

Front door

Bedroom

Bedroom

Family room

Kitchen

Patio

Deck

Property line

Existing treeline

BASE MAP

Property line

PLOT PLAN

SCALE

0   40

LOT 54

165.64

DEVELOP A BASE MAP

Mapping your property is the first step in designing a landscape plan. A base map will show property lines, existing structures, paving, and trees; anything that is going to remain the way it is will be represented on your base plan. You'll also indicate on your base map any existing trees you plan to remove. This base plan will be the foundation for other traced drawings you'll develop in later stages of the design.

Start with the plot plan prepared by a surveyor when you purchased your home. This is usually on notebook-sized paper—too small for sketching ideas. Take your plot plan to a reprographics store for enlarging. Here's what to do:

1. Take an engineer's scale with you. Make a same-size photocopy of your plot plan, preserving your original. Draw a dark 1-inch-long line in the center of your photocopy. Look at the scale of your plot plan. If one inch equals 30 feet, label your line 30 feet. If the scale of your plan is 1"= 40', label your line 40 feet. This line is necessary to check the accuracy of your enlargement.

2. Circle the drawing of your property, excluding the title and all excess space. The circled portion is the image area.

3. Ask the store to make an enlargement for you. To save money, explain that you need only the image area enlarged to fit on a 24×36 inch sheet of paper. Stress that the enlargement must be to scale. It's generally best to request 1"=10' scale.

4. Ask that the copy be made on bond paper; vellum costs more. Explain that it's okay if the enlargement is on several separate sheets of paper, as long as the image overlaps. You can tape pages together and trace a composite later.

5. Check the scale of your enlargement before leaving the shop. The 1-inch line you drew on your photocopy is now longer on your enlargement, but dimensions should still be proportional. Turn your engineer's scale to the side that matches the scale you requested. Measure your enlarged line. It should reflect the same dimension you labeled earlier. Let's say your original drawing was at a 40 scale; your 1-inch line represented 40 feet. On the reproduction at 10 scale, the line you drew should now be 4 inches long, but it still represents 40 feet. You now have a larger drawing, but all the proportions are the same. Take your enlargement home and add the measurements of existing features. This is your base plan.

You can skip this step and commission a surveyor to produce a survey at 1"=10' scale; expect to spend a few hundred dollars. If your site needs extensive grading, you will need a topography map prepared (see page 62).

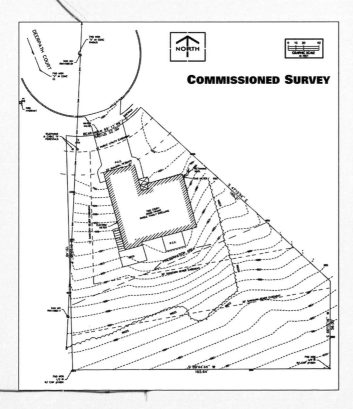

COMMISSIONED SURVEY

SPOTTING TREES

Show existing features such as trees on your base map. Use a tape measure to measure items from a fixed point shown on your plot plan. Always measure in two directions to confirm approximate locations. Use your engineer's scale to replicate these dimensions on your plan. Draw a dot to represent the trunk of each tree. Label dots if you know plant names; if not, describe with simple notes such as nice shade tree, damaged tree, or young tree. Try to remember if the tree keeps its leaves in winter or loses them and note that, too.

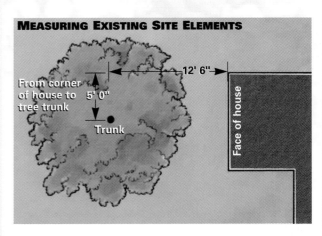

MEASURING EXISTING SITE ELEMENTS

From corner of house to tree trunk 5' 0"

12' 6"

Trunk

Face of house

IDENTIFY PROBLEMS AND ASSETS

Before: *The view from the front door was flat, plain, and focused only on neighboring houses.*

Before: *The existing deck offered a nice rear view of the woods, but the view to the side looked onto the neighbors' home. The deck needed more privacy.*

It's time to look at your property as if you were visiting for the first time. You're going to determine the existing advantages and shortcomings. This is the first step in creation of your site analysis.

Take notes of site assets and problems from front yard to back. Translate all of these observations to a "problems and assets list". Include all areas of the property—side yard, too (see the sample list on page 31). This list will form the basis of your site analysis.

A FRESH LOOK

Start with a look from the road to see the first impression your property makes. Work your way up the driveway and then to the front door. Is it clear which door guests should enter? Is the walk to that door comfortable,

convenient, and inviting or dull, colorless, and narrow? Then pay attention to the route your family takes into the house. Your landscape should welcome the people who live there each day.

TAKE PICTURES

Next, take pictures of your yard. The camera is less forgiving than your own eyes. It's easy for you to overlook things you see every day; you'll be surprised how much the photos call attention to unsightly details. It's also easier to think objectively when studying photographs.

Stand across the street and take panoramic shots of your front yard. Hold the camera at the same level while clicking shots and overlap them slightly. Be sure to include the house in the photos. Tape the developed pictures together to form a composite view of what your home looks like to neighbors and passersby. You may be surprised to discover that you can see right into your living room window. Or you may have never noticed how unattractive your garbage cans are. Sometimes making cosmetic improvements is as easy as removing that pile of scrap lumber you've come to ignore.

Take pictures of other areas of the yard, too. Pay attention to views seen from windows and exterior sitting areas. Photograph existing features as well as the areas you see as problems. Most design professionals use this technique to analyze the site and design the best solutions. It is helpful to be able to glance at a photograph of trees in your yard when working on your plans. All those dots you carefully plotted on your base map will be more useful if you have a handy visual reminder of the real thing.

Photos will help you evaluate the features of your home. Perhaps you'll see your porch is an architectural asset, but realize the side of your garage is nothing more than a blank, windowless wall. This information will help you design a landscape that will play up good features and minimize flaws.

PATHS AND ACCESS

As you study the photographs, consider access to and from your house. Do interior and exterior spaces relate? For instance, does your living room open onto an outdoor entertaining area? Is there a fresh-air dining spot close to the kitchen? Now look at routes through your landscape. Are there areas of your yard that you never visit because they are hard to reach? Is it easy to get from the front yard to the back? Are there paths leading to nowhere? Are walkways wide enough to walk two abreast? Include this information in your inventory.

DON'T FORGET YOUR ASSETS

Don't get so discouraged with the problems of your yard that you overlook its potential. Note good views, attractive plants, healthy lawn areas, spots with established privacy, level places, slopes, and areas of sun and shade in morning and afternoon. Be sure to list good features of your house, too, such as attractive windows, convenient exterior doors, chimneys, and pretty trim or rails.

Your inventory will prove valuable as you translate the flaws and opportunities of your landscape to your site analysis. This analysis is the next step in developing your plan, and it will guide you through the evolution of design ideas.

Use the list below as a guide.

Site analysis will help identify problems, such as improper drainage, steep access, and toxic weeds in natural areas.

PROBLEMS AND ASSETS LIST

Area of Yard	Problems	Assets
Front yard	Easy to pass by house, nothing distinctive about first impression Lack of color Front door seems to recede Needs foundation planting No trees—house seems too tall Run-on lawn	Healthy lawn Level yard Bay window Angled lot sets house away from neighbors (not in a row) Sunny Tidy new home has fresh look
Western side yard	Slope makes it difficult to go around house Access to deck steps through lawn, no hard surface No destination—no reason to visit the side yard No separation from neighbor's yard Lack of vertical interest; no trees and few windows on side of house	Healthy lawn Access to deck Spacious Sunny
Backyard	Underside of tall deck dominates yard Minimal sitting area Lacks interest near house—no plants except lawn No destinations—no reason to leave existing patio or deck Poison ivy in woods limits exploring Mowing a slope No privacy on western side	Excellent view: beautiful woods along back of property with good natural vegetation Existing wildlife feeding station French doors open onto existing patio Pretty view from deck off of kitchen Healthy lawn Interesting topography: level by house, sloping down to lawn and woods Privacy along three sides (north, south, and east) Southern exposure allows winter sun while house blocks winter winds No glare—do not have to look into sun to view woods Pleasantly sunny, with some shadows cast by woods Native wildflowers along edge of woods Pleasant sound of breeze through trees
Eastern side yard	Inconvenient to walk around house Excess lawn—mowing an area that isn't used	Private Plenty of room

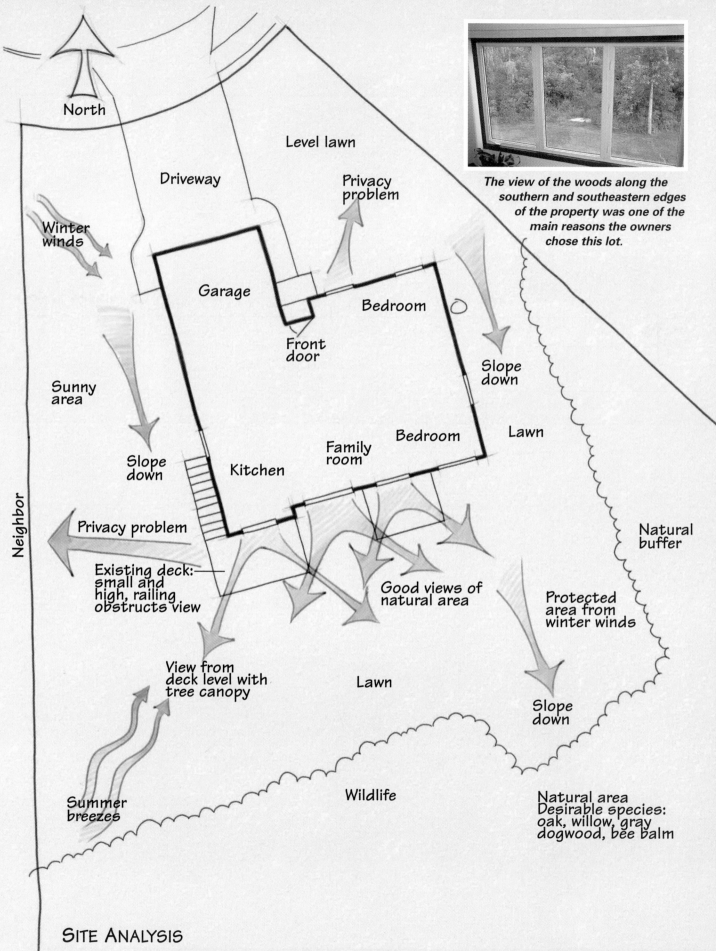

North

Driveway

Level lawn

Privacy problem

The view of the woods along the southern and southeastern edges of the property was one of the main reasons the owners chose this lot.

Winter winds

Garage

Bedroom

Front door

Slope down

Sunny area

Slope down

Kitchen

Family room

Bedroom

Lawn

Neighbor

Privacy problem

Natural buffer

Existing deck: small and high, railing obstructs view

Good views of natural area

Protected area from winter winds

View from deck level with tree canopy

Lawn

Slope down

Summer breezes

Wildlife

Natural area Desirable species: oak, willow, gray dogwood, bee balm

SITE ANALYSIS

ANALYZE YOUR SITE

Completing the inventory of problems and assets might have started you thinking about the condition of your existing landscape. Now you can transfer those thoughts to your plan to make a graphic representation of what is good and bad about your yard. This makes it easier to see what you need to consider when designing your new landscape plan.

Spread out your base map and unroll enough tracing paper to cover it. Trace existing items—property lines, the outline of your house, existing paving, structures, and trees—from your base map. This duplicate will become your site analysis. (Always keep a clean version of your base map.) Refer to our sample site analysis for examples and transfer items from the inventory to this map. Put labels on the approximate location of the condition. Use arrows to indicate patterns of access, views, and slopes, labeling each. After you've gone through your notes, take your plan outside and see if you missed anything. Add any new observations to the site analysis by writing right on the page.

Then go back inside and take a look at what you've created. For the first time, you have an emerging picture of what your yard looks like. Having a drawing of your site lets you examine your property from a bird's-eye view. Look at the relationship between spaces.

Is your parking area near the door you use most often? You may realize that you have incompatible zones of use side by side. For example, the area right outside the master bedroom is probably not the best place for a dog run. Can you see garbage cans when you sit on your patio or deck? Then you may need to move your utility area. What kind of view do you see from your front door?

Add additional notes, circles, and arrows as needed to show how existing zones of the house and yard work together or clash. Your yard may be completely lacking any definition of zones and may form, instead, a single, run-on space. Note that, as well.

The view from the front bedroom window of this home revealed a lack of interior privacy that could be greatly improved with new landscaping.

The existing walkway stopped abruptly, interrupting the link between front and back yards.

Study photos of your house and yard and transfer your observations to your site analysis. Our project needed more interesting landscaping to prevent the garage and driveway from becoming the dominant features of the home.

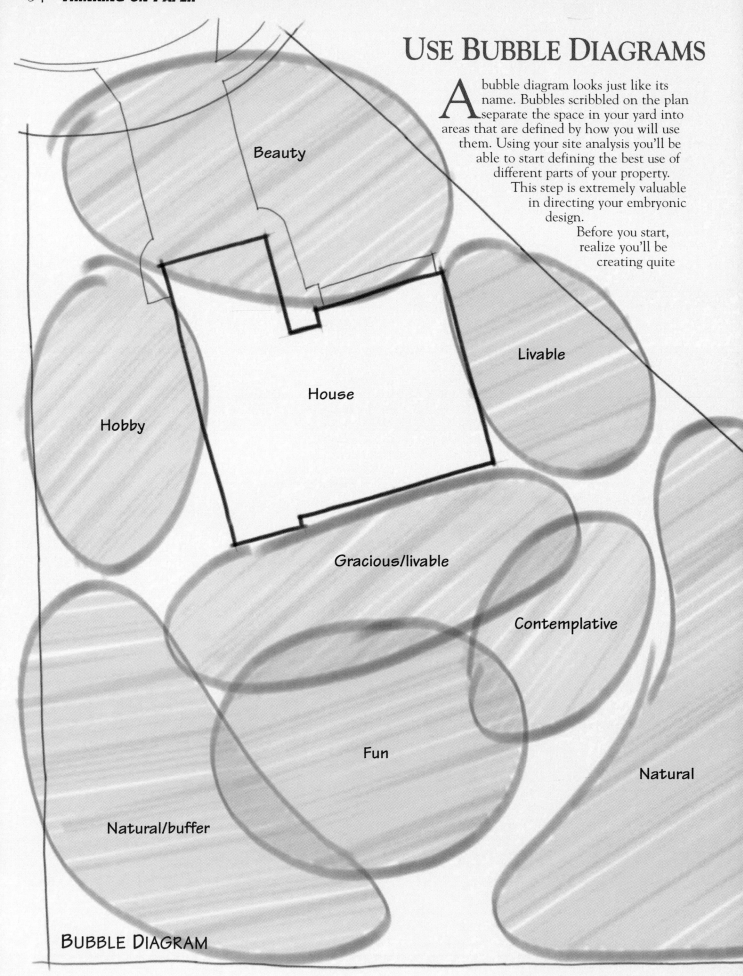

USE BUBBLE DIAGRAMS

A bubble diagram looks just like its name. Bubbles scribbled on the plan separate the space in your yard into areas that are defined by how you will use them. Using your site analysis you'll be able to start defining the best use of different parts of your property. This step is extremely valuable in directing your embryonic design.

Before you start, realize you'll be creating quite

Beauty

Livable

Hobby

House

Gracious/livable

Contemplative

Fun

Natural

Natural/buffer

BUBBLE DIAGRAM

a few bubble diagrams to consider various possibilities. Lay tracing paper over your base map and again quickly trace the basic information (property lines, house, driveway, exiting decks, patios, or walkways).

Pin your site analysis on a wall nearby so it will be a handy reference. You will find that some conditions of your property dictate that a zone be used in a specific way. Other areas will be changed to accommodate your ideas. For example, on our project, the wooded area was preserved as a natural zone. But the area immediately adjacent to the back of the house was picked as a spot to be developed for gracious living. Slide your site analysis beneath your bubble diagram to get a better idea of how your proposed uses match assets (or will solve problems) in your landscape.

DON'T BE TOO CAREFUL

Relax and expect to use a lot of tracing paper. That's the best way to draw bubble diagrams. Draw as quickly as you think. Remember, the purpose of this step is to examine relationships between proposed zones of use with each other and with existing conditions. Careful drawing takes longer, slowing down the freedom of thought and the evolution of ideas. Besides, nice drawings are hard to discard. Don't limit yourself to a particular plan just because you spent a long time drawing it. Search for the best solution.

Divide your entire site into zones. There's no hard and fast rule about what goes where, so allow yourself to experiment. Each bubble represents an area of the exterior space. Areas are defined by use, not by future content.

For example, don't try to figure out where to put a patio at this stage; decide where the best place is for an entertaining area. You may choose a spot that relates well to the inside of the house and the rest of the yard but is too steep for a patio. The solution? Build a deck, instead. If you had only looked for patio spots, you never would have considered this solution. By freeing yourself to think about the use of the area—

entertaining—you are able to discover the optimum location for this use in relation to all the other uses.

Evaluate each drawing in terms of how well each use relates to each other, to the site, and to your floor plan. Draw bubbles so they are loose and abstract, not shaped like a deck or a pool or a flower bed. Leave each finished bubble diagram in place and add another layer of tracing paper on top to try another bubble arrangement. You'll build up layers of paper as ideas evolve. You'll find it helpful to tape only the top corners of your drawings so you can lift the layers and see what you've done earlier.

THE EVOLUTION OF IDEAS

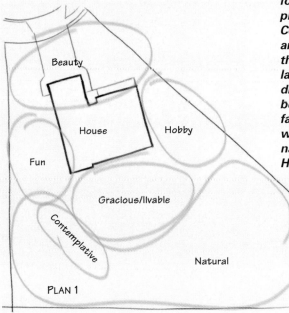

PLAN 1

PLAN 2

Rearrange bubbles to try various schemes. Evaluate your diagrams by examining how the proposed zones of use relate to your home. An early bubble diagram for our project placed the Contemplative area too close to the neighbors; a later diagram discovered a better location, facing the widest existing natural area. The Hobby zone was also relocated to the sunny side of the house for better fruit and vegetable growing conditions. The Fun area was moved from the side yard on an earlier plan to the backyard so it would take advantage of an open lawn area and relate better to the entertaining (Gracious) area.

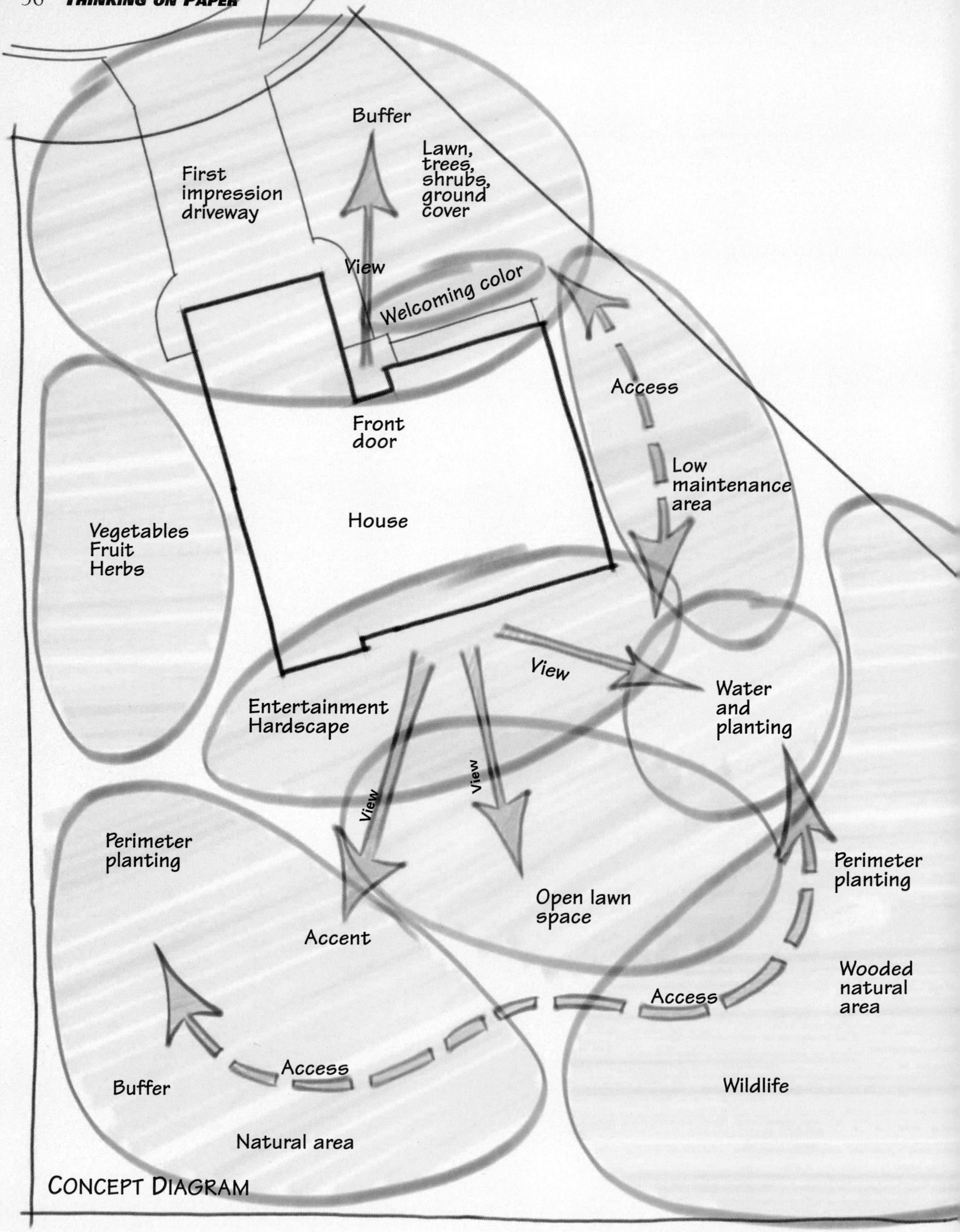

Buffer

Lawn, trees, shrubs, ground cover

First impression driveway

View

Welcoming color

Access

Low maintenance area

Front door

House

Vegetables Fruit Herbs

View

Water and planting

Entertainment Hardscape

Perimeter planting

View

View

Perimeter planting

Open lawn space

Wooded natural area

Accent

Access

Buffer

Access

Wildlife

Natural area

CONCEPT DIAGRAM

DEFINE CONCEPTS

I t's time to add another layer of detail to your plan—this time with a concept diagram. First, choose your favorite bubble diagram. Now that you've figured out what zones you want the exterior space divided into (and what purpose each area should serve), you can start applying design ideas to your spatial scheme.

It's important to still think generally. For example, you may know you want to include both hardscape and planting in your entertainment area. Note that on the appropriate bubble. You can choose among a deck, patio, or perhaps a pea-gravel terrace during the next stage, when you prepare a master plan (page 38). You will rough out shapes of plants during the next step, too, but you won't select plant species until you prepare a planting plan (page 82). You'll want to know more about plant categories (trees, shrubs, ground covers, vines, lawns, annuals, and perennials) and planting design before choosing what to buy. It's too early to be that specific.

If you've labeled an area on your concept diagram as contemplative, consider what feature works within that zone. It may be as simple as a spot to sit. On our project, we decided to add a water feature for its reflective and soothing qualities. By locating our contemplative area on the edge of the woods, we are borrowing from the site's

natural beauty but still locating it within view of the house. Water in this location will also attract wildlife. What you've done is to transform what began as a bubble scribbled on a sheet of paper into a workable plan for the creation of a peaceful sanctuary.

Jot simple notes on your concept diagram to develop similar ideas for each of your proposed zones of use.

Connect your bubbles with arrows to show where you think traffic will naturally flow, where walkways should be built, and what views need to be considered. Do your bubbles satisfy these needs? If not, you may need to rearrange them again. Remember, there's a lot of tracing paper on a roll. Use what it takes. Keep trying until you get a set of spaces you like and some rough ideas about how to fill those spaces.

Before: A healthy, level lawn was the only landscaping in front of the house, leaving plenty of room for new trees, shrubs, ground cover, and seasonal color.

Before: This snapshot, taken approximately from the future location of the water feature, shows the need for privacy on the southwestern side of the lot.

Before: This snapshot reveals the expanse of bare wall on the western side of the house, as well as the opportunity for better connection between the front drive and the rear deck.

CREATE A MASTER PLAN

Now you get to take the first step from generalities to more specific ideas. A master plan shows both hardscape and planting ideas. It is the blueprint for creating your new landscape. Don't let the thought of designing scare you; you've been designing already. Before you begin this stage, gather your written design program, your site analysis, your

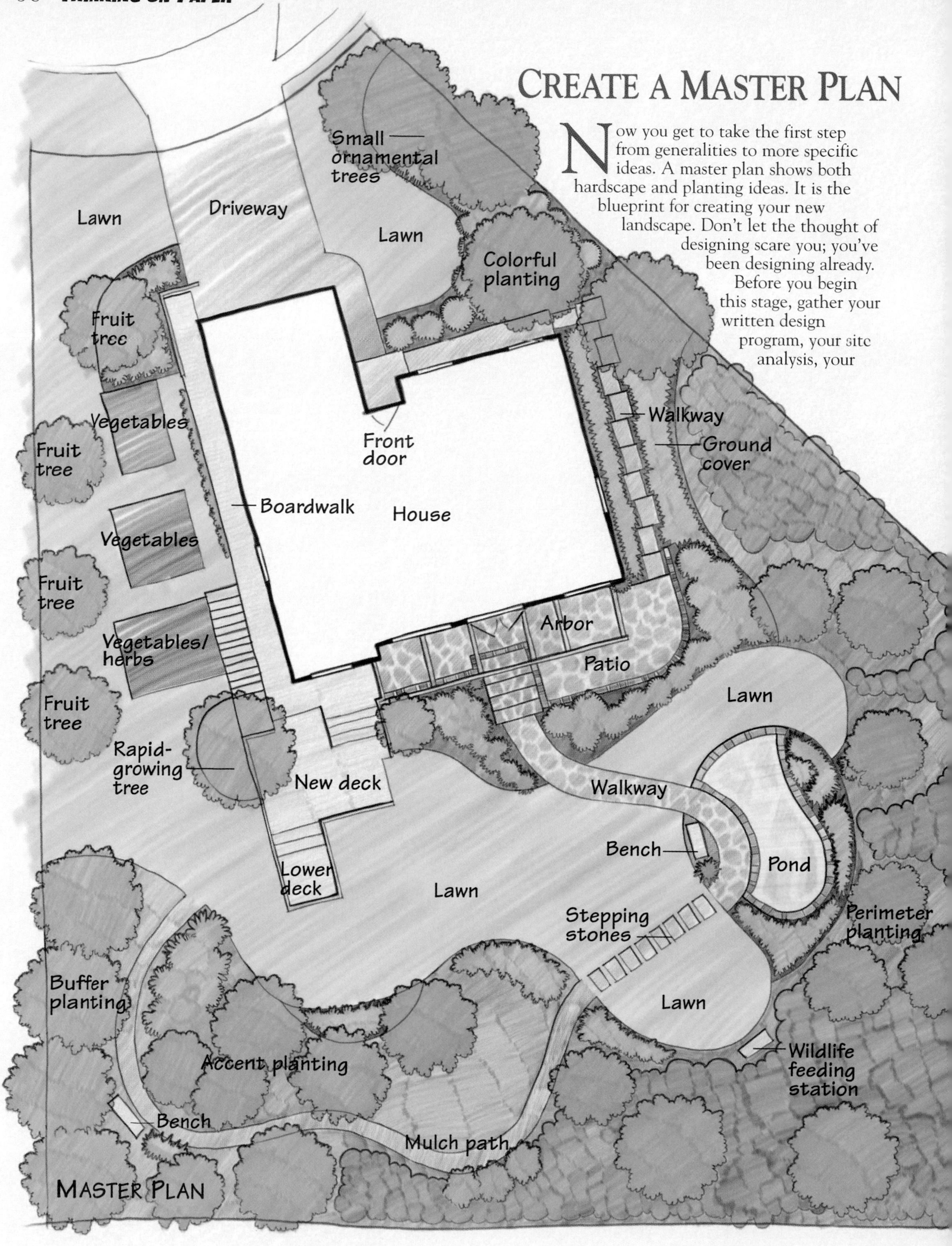

Lawn

Driveway

Small ornamental trees

Lawn

Colorful planting

Fruit tree

Vegetables

Fruit tree

Walkway

Ground cover

Vegetables

Front door

Boardwalk

House

Fruit tree

Vegetables/ herbs

Arbor

Patio

Fruit tree

Rapid-growing tree

New deck

Lawn

Walkway

Bench

Pond

Lower deck

Lawn

Stepping stones

Perimeter planting

Buffer planting

Lawn

Accent planting

Wildlife feeding station

Bench

Mulch path

MASTER PLAN

concept diagram, and the photos of your home and yard. These important reference tools will guide you in the decision-making process. Producing a master plan combines what you've learned to produce a whole. You've already done a lot of legwork on your design and probably have some definite ideas about how to use the elements and principles of design to help you solve problems.

Lay your concept diagram over your site analysis and place a clean sheet of tracing paper atop both. The combined layers of information give you a clear idea of what problems need to be solved (that blank, windowless garage wall), what assets should be celebrated (frame a pretty window with plants), how the space should be divided into zones of use, and how these zones relate to one another. Choose a zone delineated by a bubble on your concept diagram.

HARDSCAPE FIRST

Start by figuring out hardscape solutions. The underlying layers of information will help you choose locations and shapes for patios, decks, parking areas, landings, water features, and walkways. Use your engineer's scale to sketch your ideas. Plan your projects around trees you want to keep. Label trees that must be removed with an "x" in a small circle.

Examine the site analysis notes that apply to each area. Sketch out rough ideas for filling the space on your plan, as if you were in an airplane above your property looking down. Think about solutions that both meet your needs and fulfill your wishes.

If you think you want a deck, don't draw careful deck plans. Instead, play with different shapes you may want a deck to be. Be prepared to go through a trial-and-error process to come up with the best solution. But don't

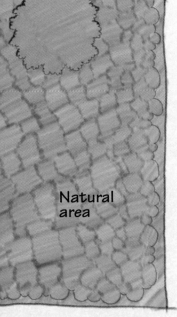

Natural area

dwell on any particular zone too long; it isn't necessary to figure out details. That will come when you produce a layout plan (page 54). Move on to another area of your site. Always take time to look at the big picture, double-checking the relationships between proposed solutions. You may find that you'd prefer to have a deck as a private retreat outside your bedroom and revert to your original patio idea for entertaining. Let your mind work though the possibilities as you rough out your ideas.

BEDLINES AND PLANTING AREAS

After you have a sketched your favorite hardscape ideas, figure out your bedlines. Wrap planting beds around hardscape items to frame them, but leave some access to grassy areas. Remember, your bedlines shape the lawn as well as planting areas. You may choose smooth, flowing curves or geometric lines (see page 18). Use your engineer's scale every now and then to check the width of planting beds. It's easy to get carried away and sketch 20-foot-wide beds that will require too many plants. Keep things workable.

Trees are next. Scribble rough circles to indicate where you want to add trees. Look at the arrows on your site analysis that indicate views you don't want to block, areas that need privacy, and areas that need shade. Consider existing trees as shown on your base map before drawing new ones.

Use your photographs as design tools so you can sketch planting areas and designate the plants you want to keep.

It's also a good idea to roughly label the floor plan of your house so you can examine the indoor/outdoor relationships. You may remember that you wanted to plant a buffer or build a fence to create more interior privacy. Make sure your hardscape ideas relate well to nearby rooms in your house.

Trace your favorite hardscape solutions and planting schemes to form a composite. This is your master plan. Even if you only implement one part of your new landscape at a time, you'll end up with a unified design with this plan.

Don't let producing a perfect drawing be your goal. Sketches are opportunities to explore ideas; shown here are several trial schemes for our pond shape.

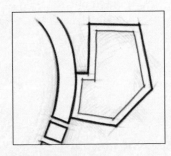

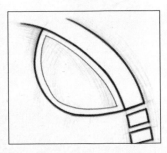

Broad stepping stones transition from paved areas to lawn. Spacing stones far enough apart allows grass to grow in between; recessing stones keeps mowing easy.

HARDSCAPE DESIGN

Anything that isn't soil or planting is considered part of your hardscape—paved surfaces, walls, fences, arbors, decks, water features, and garden amenities. You'll need layout plans to build them. But first, it's a good idea to consider some of the things that can affect their installation.

PAVING

Think of paving as the floor for outdoor rooms and hallways. The term paving describes any surface that is not planted and is suitable for walking or driving. Driveways, parking courts, walkways, sport courts, and patios are just a few examples of hardscape paving.

Paving materials vary greatly and can be broadly categorized as impermeable and permeable. Impermeable surfaces—asphalt, concrete, and brick or stone mortared to concrete slabs—are firm enough to shed storm water. These surfaces lend an air of permanence and formality.

You will usually need to hire a contractor to pave areas with impermeable materials, since the subsurface requires preparation to prevent cracking. Poured-in-place concrete requires forms to hold it in place until it has cured. Precast concrete pieces, such as stepping stones, are already hardened and ready for placement.

Permeable surfaces provide a firmer surface than the ground, but still allow water to penetrate. They give your landscape an informal tone. Gravel and mulch are common examples. If you're interested in a "middle ground," consider stone, brick, or pavers set in a sand course; they have a stronger presence than gravel or mulch. Sand-set bricks tend to shift over the years, making a surface charmingly uneven. Moss and plants may grow in pockets that occur. Permeable paving materials and sand beds need to be contained with steel, stone, brick, or wood edging.

Paving is a great way to transition from one space to another. For example, irregularly shaped stones set in a loose gravel path may lead to a patio made of the same stones mortared to a slab. A rectangular inset of cut stones centered in the patio acts much like an exterior area rug, lending subtle identity and a touch of formality to a sitting area. Examine your plan carefully for areas that will be paved and consider different materials to find the look you want.

It's important to know what you can do yourself and when it's time to call a contractor. A brick-on-sand patio project or a gravel path lined with brick or stone is within the skill of many homeowners. Straight-line shapes are easier than curves. Projects with dimensions that divide into an even number of bricks are easier than those that require bricks to be cut.

Exposed-aggregate concrete slabs give an angular edge to a lawn area and create a walkway that's wide enough for two people side by side.

Gravel isn't just for rural settings. Neatly hemmed by clipped boxwood hedges, a gravel path and seating area add texture to a formal garden. The smaller the stone, the dressier the appearance. Mixtures with fewer white stones tend to make the prettiest pathways, establishing a continuity of color.

GETTING ROUGH BIDS

Because your master plan is drawn to scale, you can measure the paved areas and calculate square footage. Obtain rough bids from several contractors to see if your plans are affordable. You may need to reduce the amount of paving or select materials that are less expensive. After you prepare a layout plan, you'll be able to determine all your costs more precisely.

COST FACTORS

The price of paving depends on the availability of materials and labor necessary for installation. Anything that requires intensive craftsmanship will cost more than a simple surface. Is the project in a difficult-to-reach backyard? Accessibility to your project area will affect the price; so will the amount of site preparation needed.

Geography makes a difference, too. What materials are most available in your area? Brick in south Florida costs more than other places; the lack of local clay for making masonry means shipping costs are necessary. Native stone may be readily available in your area. By choosing materials native to your area, you'll not only save money, but you'll also ensure that your design will achieve a look appropriate to your region.

SPECIALTY CONCRETE

Adding concrete to your landscape doesn't mean you have to settle for the same old blinding white paving. Integral color mixes added to concrete before pouring can create a range of hues. Most start off dark and fade to lighter shades, so choose a tone darker than what you ultimately want. Existing concrete can be stained with a chemical product that etches the surface for a pleasingly mottled look. Adding shells or decorative stone into the wet mix and hosing an unset surface to expose aggregates gives concrete an interesting texture. Closed-mold stamps used on the surface of wet concrete can create amazing patterns that suggest cobblestones, bricks, or rocks.

A dark gravel parking area is an example of permeable paving. In this design, a mortared cobblestone edge contains the gravel. The combination is both tidy and consistent with the rustic charm of the home.

Brick is an excellent material for adding rich color and pattern to your landscape. Here, a herringbone brick terrace (foreground) is separated by header-course steps that lead down to a running bond walkway. The header course continues as a band around the walk. The changes in patterns correspond to changes in elevation.

Cut stones give paved areas a touch of formality. This pattern, which mixes square and rectangular stones of similar sizes, is called random ashlar.

DECKS

There's nothing quite as versatile as a deck. You can add outdoor living space adjacent to any floor of your house, over slopes and ravines, nestled in the trees, or right at ground level. A deck can make the most of views, summer breezes, and winter sunshine. Like paving, decks and boardwalks form the floors of outdoor rooms and passageways. But unlike paving, decks give you the option of building above ground, and grading is rarely necessary.

LOCATION

A second-story deck can take advantage of wasted space despite rugged terrain. Always check local building codes for rail specifications before building.

Access, comfort, and privacy are all important factors in deck design. Double-check your concept diagram for the optimum location. If you have trouble getting to your deck, you'll rarely use it. Your deck is a destination; study the best ways to access it. If you feel that you are on display or the location of the deck is too hot or cold, you won't enjoy it much. You may need new planting for increased privacy or shade.

Consider how you will use your deck. Make sure the shape and size shown on your master plan will meet your needs. A small, cozy deck can be perfect for an intimate spot just off the master bedroom; a place for outdoor entertaining may require more room.

FEATURES AND COSTS

Storage can be a valuable feature. A deck beside a kitchen garden may include storage for garden tools and harvest baskets; a deck that doubles as a landing for the front or back door is an ideal spot for hooks and shelves. Built-in benches and planters make a deck more useful. Features such as lighting, overhead fans, exterior outlets, and outdoor cook tops and sinks should be planned from the beginning, even if they are added later.

It's often a good idea to add a focal point in the yard that aligns with the main view from the deck; mark these spots on your master plan. Strategically placed decorative benches, sundials, or bird feeders enhance the view.

Generally, decks are one of the most affordable hardscape options. Redwood, cedar, and pressure-treated pine are usual materials; check with local suppliers to see which is the best value in your region. You can build a deck yourself or hire a carpenter to do the work for you. Research local building codes and have underground utilities marked before footings are dug.

Use your engineer's scale to make adjustments now. You'll soon produce an accurately dimensioned drawing called a layout plan based on the footprint of the deck you design now.

CONSTRUCTION TIPS

■ Lay deck planks bark side up to prevent cupping. Examine end grain of lumber for proper positioning.
■ Nails, joist hangers, and other fasteners should be hot-dipped galvanized steel to prevent rusting. Check product labels.
■ Planks should be butt-jointed. Unless lumber is kiln-dried, shrinking will occur. Leave no spaces between planks during construction.

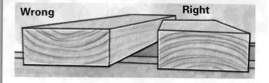

Wrong   Right

ARBORS

Arbors represent doorways and ceilings in the outdoor world. Compare your master plan to your concept diagram. Do you need more delineation between zones of use? An arbor may be just the thing you need to suggest a passageway from one area of your yard to another.

Adding an arbor to your garden can also give it presence and style. A simple, two-post structure is perfect for framing the entry into your garden. Larger arbors with multiple posts make big spaces feel comfortable. Most interior ceilings are 8 to 9 feet high; bringing that height outside with an overhead structure can make large exterior spaces seem people-sized. As a rule of thumb, include beams or rafters within those heights and the proportions will feel comfortable.

By studying the angle of the fiercest rays the area receives, you can slant rafters to block bright sun. You may need only a few rafters if the purpose of the arbor is to define space. The sight of the structure within the yard signals that the area designated is special.

Large, multiple-post arbors create outdoor rooms by suggesting the skeletal framework of doorways and overhead ceilings. Climbing vines can shade sitting areas.

DESIGN FOR STYLE

Arbor construction varies with design intent. Curved arbors contribute a romantic quality to the garden; white arches covered with climbing roses establish the cottage style. Repeating the bottom half of the arch along the top of a gate completes the circle. Known as moon gates, these arbor-gate combinations frame porthole views of the area beyond them. Position a focal point so that it can be seen while looking through the circle; this point of interest doesn't have to be centered like a target. Consider setting it slightly to one side to balance the geometric shape of the moon gate. A curving path, leading invitingly to some unseen destination, is another good view to frame.

Rectilinear arbors without curves make a different statement in your landscape. Consider repeating the peak of your rooftop or the horizontal line of your fence top. Whether the style becomes formal or informal depends largely upon the materials and colors you use. Dressed and painted lumber suggests a formal presence. Rough cedar posts lend a rustic air. You can also combine stone or brick pillars with wood or iron to form a gateway planted with trailing vines. Design an arbor to reflect your own personal style and to complement the architecture of your home.

A moon gate arbor and mantle of roses sends the message that when you enter this garden you will be stepping into a special place.

A brick wall makes a below-street-level garden feel secluded. The wall stops the sight line and forms a solid background, showcasing a bold sculpture. The smooth surface of the artwork and its pedestal contrast with the textures of bricks and vines.

Tall enough to block outside views and ornate enough to decorate the garden, this custom wall repeats the hues of the floral color scheme, yet stands out from the planting with its architectural detail. The angled cap sheds water, extending the life of the lumber.

Dry-stacked (unmortared) stone walls are perfect for a cottage or rustic look. Freestanding walls are usually wider at the base for greater stability. Retaining walls lean backwards into the slope for support. Weep holes aren't necessary as water can seep between stones.

WALLS AND FENCES

Walls and fences claim a corner of earth for your own. You can make walls for outdoor rooms, to limit access, and to direct the flow of foot traffic.

Lay your master plan over your site analysis to help you see where you need to add buffers for privacy, to define space, or to keep children and pets from straying.

DESIGN WITH WALLS

The solid form of most walls lends a sense of permanence. Age a new landscape by building a wall with old materials; it will seem to have always been there. Planting vines to creep over it marries a wall to the garden. Tall walls can appear imposing, adding a hint of exclusiveness or creating an air of mystery by piquing curiosity about what is out of view. Walls taller than eye-level can seem forbidding and unfriendly when built next to a sidewalk with no planting between.

Walls don't have to be tall; they can be less than a foot high. A low line of stacked stones makes an effective area divider; a short wall topped with a picket fence makes a clearly defined boundary that doesn't obscure views. The line the wall follows influences the style of your landscape; a wall that meanders has an informal flair. Walls that follow predictable paths add a formal touch.

Walls may be made of stone, brick, adobe, concrete, stucco, or any combination of materials. To cut costs, construct walls of concrete block and cover the face with a decorative veneer. When planning to build a wall, you must take legal restrictions into consideration. Remember that walls need footings which may extend beyond its width on both sides—make sure you have room.

FENCING WITH A FLAIR

Fences offer even more style variations than walls. Waist-high picket fences add cottage charm and define space without seeming unfriendly. Tall privacy fences screen unwanted views or create privacy. Rustic fences can suggest a cabin or countryside setting. Fences may be made of wood, wire, or metal. Choose one or combine materials to get the look and level of maintenance you want. Decide whether you want to completely block views or merely add a sense of separation from surrounding areas.

Remember, you don't have to use one type of wall or fence around your entire property. Consider repeating materials to create unity, but vary heights to serve different purposes.

LIVING FENCES

You can combine fences or walls with hedges for a different kind of boundary. Build corners and segments of fencing and plant shrubs in between. Thorny plants make an effective barrier; flowering plants add a decorative touch. Depending on the density and eventual height of the shrubs used you can achieve a range of effects, from a high enclosure surrounding an estate to a charming hedge fronting a bungalow.

About 30- to 36-inches high, painted bright white, and planted with roses, the classic picket fence adds friendly charm to the landscape. It's tall enough to keep stray children and pets from wandering through planting beds but low enough for conversation.

A couple of coats of paint can turn a similar fence into a statement of personal style. This distinctive color complements the dominant hue of the flower scheme and brightens the winter landscape, too.

Open metal fencing supported by masonry pilasters forms a long-lasting fence. The sturdy pillars have an imposing air that is softened by the open metal work which permits views within.

A low lattice fence is all that's needed to define the edge of a garden and separate a pathway from a planting bed. Short enough to step over, the fence nonetheless gives the message that routes are to be adhered to.

A six-foot-high stockade fence forms a barrier for privacy. Stockade fences can be custom-built or made from prefabricated sections. Shadowbox fences, with alternating pickets on each side of the fence, are equally attractive. It's a good idea to set fence posts in concrete footers to support the weight of sections.

Split-rail fences are easy to build and add a rustic charm to your property. Left to weather naturally, split-rail fences are good choices for separating natural areas from maintained garden areas. They're also appropriate beside pasture land and around country-style kitchen gardens.

WATER FEATURES

For adults, there are two main types of water features: water you look at and water you get into. Children frequently and willfully fail to make the distinction. Make any water feature both pretty enough to admire and safe enough for small adventurers.

Study your master plan and site analysis to see where you may want to add the sound of water to mask outside noises and enhance privacy. Look for spots that need focal points, too. Some water features, such as garden ponds, can add a contemplative quality to your landscape. Other options—splashing fountains or swimming pools—can add activity to an area. Design the water feature you want to match the use of the area.

SAFETY FIRST

Always consult local building codes for safety and liability information before adding any outdoor water feature. Fencing, wiring, lighting, and water depth may all be subject to local regulations.

A tiered fountain is an ornate addition to this water feature. With the coping clearly visible, the pond design does not attempt to imitate a woodland pond, making the formal fountain an appropriate choice.

PONDS AND WATERFALLS

Garden ponds are popular ways to bring water to the landscape. The sight of water has a cooling effect in summer. A dark bottom enhances the reflective qualities; that's why pond liners are usually black. Sold in kits, these durable plastic sheets conform to any shape. There are also rigid, preformed basins in many shapes.

Ponds can be naturalistic or elegant and formal. If a natural pond is your goal, obscure liner edges with stones, wood, or plants. For a formal look, build a raised geometric coping.

Splashes, gurgles, and falling water make a garden come to life.

Good design can make a swimming pool a feature of your landscape instead of merely a place for activity. Tinting the concrete finish slightly avoids motel-blue water and adds a touch of elegance.

Waterfalls can be built from kits with pumps that return the water from a pool to the top for an ongoing flow. Waterfalls look best when integrated into the landscape. A pile of wet rocks in the center of the yard isn't as naturally striking as stones set on a slope that's lush with ferns and iris. Pay attention to what's behind your waterfall; screen distractions so your water feature will stand out.

FOUNTAINS ADD SPLASH

Fountains offer a chance to incorporate water in your landscape without the expense or space of a large pool. A wall-mounted fountain adds sparkle to the sight and music to the air. Small bubblers can add movement to garden ponds. Fountains flowing into pools can be made of anything from ornate cast iron to broken pottery.

Whether you want a formal or naturalistic look for your pond, make it clearly one style or the other. An irregular shape, stone coping, dark bottom, and abundant water plants combine to help this garden pond successfully mimic one that's natural.

Use your imagination to discover how everyday materials—urns, galvanized feeding troughs, watering cans—can help create a water feature. Work with an electrician to connect your pump to its power source; include a ground-fault interrupter in all water features. You can set fountains and waterfalls on timers so they will only run when you are likely to be home.

POOLSIDE BEAUTY

A swimming pool doesn't have to be a big blue hole in your landscape. Consider it as a large water feature that will complement the space when not in use. Any pool can be pretty enough for sitting even if you have no plans to swim. Add a stone patio with an arbor and lush plantings, and it becomes a focal point for even the most formal gathering. The sound of gently splashing water makes the pool even more inviting; consider building small jets into the side of a swimming pool to turn a plain wall into a row of arching spouts. Or direct a flow of recirculating water over a pool lip and down into a hidden trough for a poolside waterfall.

The location of your swimming pool plays a part in its appeal, too. Don't plop it in the center of the back lawn where it dominates. Tuck it along one side, connect it to your bedroom, curve it around existing plants; list as many options as you can before planning where to excavate. You'll also want to allow room for pool equipment, and you'll want to screen it from view.

Is a swimming pool what you really want? If swimming laps isn't what you had in mind, perhaps a spa would be a better use of your space and resources. An in-ground spa or raised deck can attractively house a prefabricated model.

At first, the long stones set in the water seem part of a natural configuration. But a stepping-stone path leading to the water's edge reveals some clever planning. Consider making your garden pond or pool a part of the landscape circulation instead of a dead end.

PLANTS, FISH, FILTERS, AND PUMPS

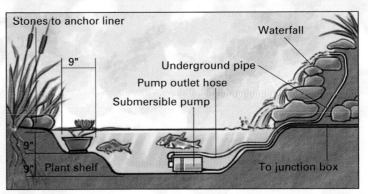

Plants for ponds must be chosen carefully. Hardy waterlilies will fare better in most climates than tropical varieties. Set waterlilies and other water-loving plants such as umbrella plant (*Cyperus alternifolius*) in containers on shallow shelves built into the sides of your pond. Avoid puncturing pond liners or basins when you install plants. Iris, rushes, and ferns are good choices to plant beyond the pond's edge.

Fish add color and movement to the water. Always purchase fish from a reputable source and never free exotic fish in local waterways, where they may become invasive. Include water plants in your pond so fish can hide from predators. Fish are cold-blooded and can survive the winter outdoors if the surface of the water is not allowed to freeze solid, depriving them of oxygen.

Filters help keep ponds clean but may not be necessary in a properly balanced ecosystem—some carefully designed systems rely on the roots of water plants to naturally filter pond water.

Pumps are either remote or submersible. Most garden ponds utilize small submersible pumps that sit on the pond bottom. Pumps keep water recirculating which helps the pond stay healthy. Pump sizes are dependent upon the desired flow and the height water will have to ascend to a waterfall. Many pond kits come complete with pumps properly sized.

The geometric shape, exposed coping, and paved surrounding area make this pond a formal feature in the landscape.

Add an arbor where you want to mark an entrance into the garden or link garden rooms. An arbor adds structure to the landscape, balancing the softer lines and billowing forms of plants. It also adds a vertical element, making the scene more than just beds of flowers at ground level.

GARDEN AMENITIES

A landscape is as much fun to decorate as a house. You should, of course include ornamental items as a part of your design. But too much "stuff" can result in cluttered chaos. Use the design principles—balance, unity, and accent—to make your decorations striking.

BALANCE, UNITY, AND ACCENT

You can achieve balance in different ways. A symmetrical grouping of hand-thrown pots will divide itself neatly into identical halves. For an asymmetrical arrangement, group small pots beside a big one.

Balance is also a matter of relating a piece to the space around it. If a lion's head fountain is too small in relation to its surrounding wall, the fountain will get lost. You could choose to buy a larger fountain, but what if you particularly want to use the small one? Train a plant to grow flat against the wall—a technique known as espalier—to provide an intermediate matte to balance the object with its setting. Then the fountain no longer appears out of scale.

Understanding different unifying techniques can give you new ideas. Alternating the same large and small terra-cotta pots on the ledge is an example of rhythm. Stagger the pots from largest to smallest—that's sequence. For design with repetition, use the terra-cotta color elsewhere in the scene by echoing the hue in the stain on an arbor.

Outdoor pavilions and gazebos are garden amenities that double as focal points and outdoor destinations. Because they are usually tall enough to be seen from anywhere in the landscape, take care to locate them carefully to avoid competing with other accent features.

Place accent items where the composition needs pizzazz. Don't always aim for eye level; unexpected accents placed high or low keep a design dynamic. Rusted relics, architectural fragments, salvaged items, and antique tools find new life as garden accessories. Keep in mind that it is the position of an article that makes it an accent. Contrast the color, texture, line, or form of an item with its setting to make it noticeable.

A bright Mexican tile can add a colorful accent where you need one, but where not needed, it could be an unwanted distraction. A layer of coarse-textured river rock can serve as a foreground to a planting bed; too much rock could upset the balance of texture.

A LITTLE SOMETHING EXTRA

Furniture is an amenity that's also functional. Even a landscape designed for a lot of family activity needs a place for repose. No matter how lovely your courtyard may be, if there isn't a comfortable and convenient place to

Outdoor seating is a valuable addition that can make your landscape more attractive and more useful. Plan ahead to include room for benches, chairs, tables, umbrellas, or swings. Screens for privacy, paving, and colorful plants will help make your seating area appealing.

sit, you probably won't spend time there. There are benches and table-and-chair sets of all styles to choose from, but don't stop there. Swings, rocking chairs, and hammocks also offer rest, and they introduce a relaxing form of movement.

Vertical structures offer all sorts of design solutions. Arbors (see page 43) serve as doorways and suggest a division of space. A gazebo can add a distinct focal point to an outdoor room and make the landscape usable in wet weather by providing a dry, comfortable place to sit and watch rain fall. Storage sheds can do more than keep clutter out of sight; properly positioned, a shed can increase privacy by blocking views.

Paint doesn't need to be limited to interior walls. Color can help camouflage utilitarian items, such as meters and irrigation risers. Black is often the best; it tends to recede. Muted shades of olive green and brown are effective, too, but avoid bright greens. Artificial colors stand out among natural greenery and may ambush your camouflage attempts.

Bright paint colors can add eye-catching accents. Furniture and fences are easy canvases for brushing on color. Picket fences are traditionally painted white to make them a noticeable decorative element. But if your fence is intended to serve as a background for your composition, a dark or neutral paint or stain may be a better choice.

Movement in a landscape indicates activity, like balloons at a birthday party. Incorporating water is an excellent way to keep a space from becoming static and dull; swimming fish and falling water add motion (see page 46). Wind chimes, weather vanes, and some sculptures react to breezes flowing through an area. Wildlife can add movement that comes and goes; feeders and houses combined with habitat and food source plants will attract birds to your landscape. Planting host plants and nectar-bearing flowers will attract butterflies as well as hummingbirds to grace your yard.

THINK AHEAD

Most garden amenities should be planned in advance. You may decide to widen a pathway to provide a solid surface to house a bench. Sculpture and interesting plant forms may need night lighting for maximum enjoyment. Moving water requires a power source. All of these considerations should be addressed during this part of the planning stage. Later, after your new landscape has become reality, you'll enjoy adding a few additional accessories as finishing touches to your outdoor rooms.

Before you add a shed, decide whether you want to highlight it as a feature or downplay its appearance. Bright paint, flowers, weather vanes, and hanging relics make sheds stand out. Dark, neutral paints and stains, evergreen plantings, and less prominent placement can make your shed subordinate to the rest of your landscape.

The placement of amenities is critical. A bench can be a pleasant surprise, tucked into the landscape along a solitary path. The same bench, when placed prominently in a different composition, becomes a focal point, as in this sheltered seating area.

Containers are an easy and inexpensive way to accessorize your landscape. Set potted plants in planting beds for extra emphasis. Here, a handful of flowers is elevated to accent status by the height and colors of its container.

MATERIALS COMPARISON

As you choose materials for the hardscape elements in your design, you'll want to consider other factors associated with each. Listed below are various materials that can be used in hardscape construction, with relative comparisons of their costs, maintenance requirements, life expectancy, and the skill level required for their installation. The ratings are approximate, and some factors, such as cost and life expectancy, will vary from region to region.

FENCES AND ARBORS

There are several choices of fencing material. Each retailer may represent different manufacturers, so spend some time visiting lumberyards and home centers before making your decision. Ask to see brochures from the different manufacturers. These are packed with information about materials available as well as tips for installation and maintenance. You should weigh cost, appearance, and maintenance qualities in making your decision. Determine if beauty or barrier is more important to you. Chain link and stockade fencing are the most secure, but the least attractive. Conversely, picket and split rail models are beautiful, but they aren't very effective at keeping animals or people in—or out of—your yard. The chart below lists several things you should consider when choosing materials and ranks them on a scale of 1 (least or shortest) to 5 (most or longest).

Type	Cost	Maintenance	Life	Security	Skill Level Required
Chain link	4	1	5	5	4
Picket (prefabricated sections)					
Cedar	4	3	3	2	2
Pressure-treated pine	3	3	4	2	2
Stockade (prefabricated sections)					
Pressure-treated pine	2	5	4	5	4
Cedar	2	3	2	5	4
Split rail					
Oak	2	1	3	1	1
Cedar	2	1	4	1	1
Woven					
Pine	3	5	2	3–5	5
Cedar	5	3	4	3–5	5
Lattice	1	3	1	1–2	2

WALLS

Walls are most commonly built of masonry but can also be lattice structures or made from other materials. For comparisons on wooden materials, see the chart above for fences and arbors. All walls need regular maintenance to preserve their beauty and increase their life. The main enemies of masonry work are water and ice. Regular maintenance will revolve around keeping these invaders out. When choosing a stone material, ask your supplier which types are readily available locally. You'll also want to gather information about maintenance schedules and sealants. The chart below lists several things you should consider when choosing materials and ranks them on a scale of 1 (least or shortest) to 5 (most or longest).

Type	Cost	Maintenance	Life	Skill Level Required
Concrete block with veneer				
Brick face	4	1	5	5
Irregular stone face	4	1	5	5
Cut stone face	5	1	5	5
Interlocking units	3	1	5	4
Dry-stacked stone wall	2	3	4	3

PAVING

The materials used for paving range from simple stepping stones to manufactured stone composite pavers; prices vary greatly. As with walls, using local natural material is often the least expensive option and may tie in nicely with existing walls, or stone or brickwork on your house. Flagstone and shale are common choices but can be slippery on slopes. Pavers are quickly becoming the material of choice because of their durability, beauty, and low cost. In all cases, the life of the paving system you use will be determined most by the degree to which you properly prepare the area in which the stones are laid. The chart below lists several things you should consider when choosing materials and ranks them on a scale of 1 (least or shortest) to 5 (most or longest).

Type	Cost	Maintenance	Life	Skill Level Required
Stepping stones (local stone, shale, or limestone)	2	1	5	3
Stone mortared to a slab	5	2	5	5
Brick				
In sand	3	3	4	4
Mortared to a slab	5	1	5	5
Interlocking pavers	3	1	5	4
Concrete				
Natural	2	1	5	4
Tinted				
Integral color	3	1	5	4
Stained	3	1	5	4
Stamped	4	1	5	5
Asphalt	2	2	4	5
Decomposed granite/pea gravel	1	4	2	1
Mulch	1	4	2	1

DECKS

Solid wood products, such as redwood, cedar, and pressure-treated lumber, have been the choice of deck experts for many years—but that is changing. More varieties of composite materials are being offered every year. Composite materials may be wood by-products (wood chips or flakes), wood and plastic combinations, or 100 percent plastic (often recycled). These materials have an extremely long life, due to their rot and insect resistance. You may need to use lumber for the supports and joists, however, because composites are usually not strong enough to support the weight of deck structures. The chart below lists several things you should consider when choosing materials and ranks them on a scale of 1 (least or shortest) to 5 (most or longest).

Type	Cost	Maintenance	Life	Skill Level Required
Redwood	5	1	5	4
Cedar	4	1	4	4
Pressure-treated pine	2	4	3	4
Composite wood	3	1	5	4

PLANS OF ACTION

Now that you've created a master plan showing planting and hardscape areas as well as major garden amenities, it's time to think about turning your dreams into physical realities. You'll do that with working drawings—plans that show dimensions and locations, specify plants and materials, and how you want to shape the land. Which of the following working drawings you will need to prepare will depend entirely on the complexity of your project.

Design changes—known as field adjustments—do occur during implementation. You may discover that underground rock keeps you from digging a footing. Or perhaps the back door is 6 inches further to the left than you thought. Good working drawings will help minimize the impact field adjustments have on your design.

FOUR TYPES OF WORKING DRAWINGS

A *layout plan* shows the location, dimensions, and the materials used in the construction of additions to your landscape—driveways, decks, patios, pools, walkways, parking courts, and gazebos, for example. Without your own layout plan, your walk may not line up the way you want or your deck may not be the right size. Even if you are providing the labor yourself, it's a good idea to prepare a layout plan to guide construction.

A *grading and drainage plan* directs earth work necessary before hardscape and planting can begin. This plan is prepared after the layout plan so that the earth can be shaped to accommodate your design ideas. The level of detail on this plan is dependent on the complexity of your design, your existing terrain (steep sites may require more grading), and any existing drainage problems that need to be resolved.

A *planting plan* converts the general ideas of your master plan into instructions for getting the work done. Specific plant species, sizes, spacing, and locations are shown on the planting plan. You can make a list and shop from this plan; you can also take it outside with you to figure out what goes where.

A *maintenance plan* can help you formulate ideas that will save you time for years to come. Study your master plan so you can find short cuts on chores that won't sacrifice the quality of your design.

MATERIAL AND COST ESTIMATES

Preparing working drawings will enable you to come up with a good idea of materials needed to build your new landscape. You can measure hardscape areas on your drawings and calculate square footage. You can count the plants you'll need to buy. You can determine the length of fences and walls by using your engineer's scale.

Examining your plan and listing the materials needed is called preparing a take-off. This step is essential for estimating expenses before you begin spending money. If you want help estimating costs, ask a few contractors to bid on the job. Estimates based on detailed plans will result in comparable bids. You may find that you would prefer to hire one of them to do all or part of the job for you.

Estimating expenses is important. You don't want to run out of funds when the job is incomplete. Plan ahead if you're going to allocate money as your budget allows. Phasing the project in this manner is the best way to implement your ideas in steps without having to stop unexpectedly.

SHOULD YOU HIRE A CONTRACTOR?

You can skip working drawings and rely on a contractor to work from your master plan, but beware of inherent pitfalls. Designs are often refined during the working drawing stage. It is easier to make decisions about revisions on paper than when you have a muddy mess in your front yard. If you're doing the work yourself, you may require fewer details, but figure out as much as you can on paper before investing money or spending time behind a shovel. You may find that you need to hire an expert for certain portions of the job or that you can do more than you previously thought.

You can also hire a landscape architect or garden designer to make working drawings. Provide them with a copy of your master plan and discuss your goals with them. You can also turn to a good carpenter, mason, or reputable contractor to help with construction details.

CRITICAL PATH

Work flow is part of the critical path that must be followed to build your project. Examine the order of construction as it applies to your design. Can materials be delivered close to the related work area? Will working on one part of the project block access to another? Is there adequate space for a temporary holding area for materials? Look for ways to reduce construction man-hours on the job to cut costs. Doing things in the proper order will prevent subcontractors from damaging each other's work and spending time on repairs. Though it may be preferable to complete the front yard before starting on the back, you may get a better price by having your front walk and back patio poured at the same time. Talk to your contractors to understand their needs and pricing strategies. Make a timeline to direct the work schedule, even if you are doing it yourself.

MAKING PROGRESS—A CHECKLIST FOR WORKING DRAWINGS

RESEARCH

Learning the local regulations now gives you a chance to modify your master plan for compliance before working on design specifics. Incorporate any revisions necessary in your working drawings. Check with these groups:

- ■ Local building department for codes and permits
- ■ Local zoning department for restrictions and permits
- ■ Any boards, including homeowner and neighborhood associations, that may have to review your design prior to installation

WORKING DRAWINGS

These plans need to be produced to guide estimating, bidding, and implementation:

- ■ Layout Plan
- ■ Grading and Drainage Plan
- ■ Planting Plan
- ■ Maintenance Plan

PROFESSIONAL ASSISTANCE

Consult a professional if you need help preparing working drawings yourself or if you want someone else to produce the plans for you. Here's where to turn:

- ■ For design, grading, and construction advice: landscape architect
- ■ For planting design, plant selection, and planting advice: landscape architect, garden designer, nurseryman
- ■ For construction advice: carpenter, mason, electrician, plumber, paving contractor, pool contractor, landscape contractor, irrigation contractor

PERMITS AND CODES

Always check with zoning and regulation boards to determine which codes you must comply with and what permits they require. It may be necessary to revise your design to achieve compliance. Don't forget to check restrictions set by homeowner's associations. Stopping in the middle of a project to request a variance is no fun, and boards of review may not meet on a regular basis, stalling your progress. Permits usually incur some expense, so plan ahead to include these costs in your budget.

With a well-designed layout plan, you're well on your way to building decks, patios, and the other hardscape elements in your landscape.

TIMELINE

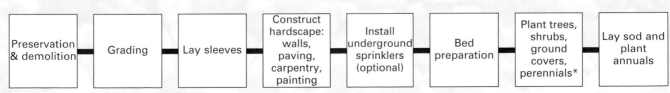

Preservation & demolition → Grading → Lay sleeves → Construct hardscape: walls, paving, carpentry, painting → Install underground sprinklers (optional) → Bed preparation → Plant trees, shrubs, ground covers, perennials* → Lay sod and plant annuals

Note: Plants should be mulched as they are installed to help them retain moisture.

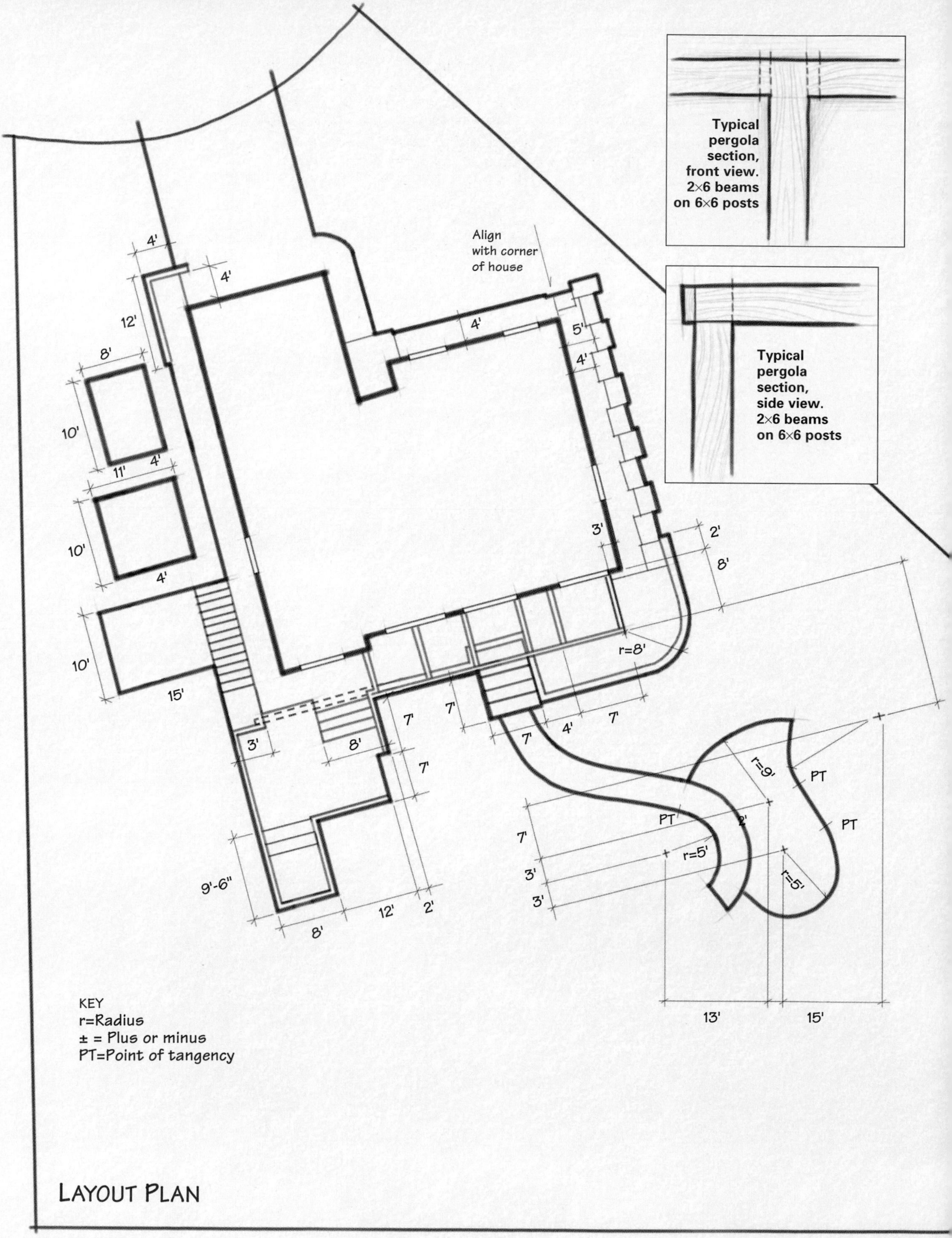

Typical pergola section, front view. 2×6 beams on 6×6 posts

Typical pergola section, side view. 2×6 beams on 6×6 posts

Align with corner of house

4'

4'

12'

8'

10'

11' 4'

10'

4'

10'

15'

3'

8'

4'

9'-6"

12' 2'

8'

4'

5'

4'

3' 2'

8'

r=8'

7' 7'

7'

7'

7' 4' 7'

7'

3'

3'

7'

r=9'

PT

PT

2'

r=5'

PT

r=5'

13' 15'

KEY
r=Radius
± = Plus or minus
PT=Point of tangency

LAYOUT PLAN

LAYOUT PLAN

A layout plan shows the outline of new hardscape items, such as decks, patios, walkways, and arbors. Don't worry if you don't have any drafting skills. Your master plan, roll of tracing paper, engineer's scale, and a couple of pencils, felt-tip pens, and a good eraser are all you need.

Using a fat, felt-tip pen, start by tracing the outline of proposed hardscape items and existing features. Don't show proposed plants or existing plants you plan to remove; *do* include major existing plants (such as trees and large shrubs) that you plan to keep. You will want to make your new hardscape features conform to what is already there so you don't have to cut down valuable trees.

DIMENSION LINES

Next, draw dimension lines in pencil, bracketed on each end (they look like an elongated "H"), with the measurement in the center. (If you try to note them directly on

each feature on your plan, your drawing will quickly become crowded and illegible.) Draw dimension lines to show how far new items will be from existing features. Next, use your engineer's scale to measure the distances indicated by your dimension lines. Use the layout plan at left for reference.

CRITICAL AND ADJUSTABLE MEASUREMENTS

When measuring, focus on one new feature at a time. Some dimensions will be more critical than others. For example, if you plan a deck designed around an existing tree, the deck must be correctly sized to fit properly. Measure the deck starting from the tree.

Other dimensions can be adjusted to make the more critical dimensions work. Label these measurements with a plus-or-minus (±) sign. For example, the length of the deck from the tree to the house is less critical. Placing the plus-or-minus symbol in front of this measurement indicates that the deck must reach from the tree to the house, but the exact length is subject to adjustment. This technique conveys your desires to the contractor. If you show the length of the deck from house to tree at exactly 24 feet, you may come home to find that your tree has been cut down in order to make room for the deck.

CONSIDER USES

Consider how you will use your new landscape. If you are going to place an umbrella table with chairs on a proposed patio, set up the actual furniture and measure the space required. Don't forget to measure the spread of the umbrella so you will allow for clearance. If your patio is not a dead-end destination, people will walk across it to get from one place to another; you'll need to allow room for the furniture area off to one side to access a walkway.

MAKE CHANGES

Don't be afraid to adjust your design as needed to make it fit your site and your needs. If you change your design, sketch the changes in pencil on top of your felt-tip outline. If things get confusing, add another layer of tracing paper to make a composite sketch.

A layout plan is a great chance to refine your design and improve your ideas. Preparing a layout plan is part of the ongoing design process; by combining your dreams with reality, the layout plan allows you to come up with creative solutions you will enjoy long after they are implemented.

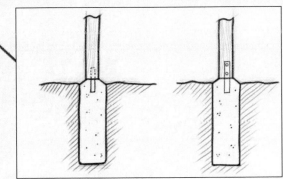

Deck post and footing detail. 4×4 posts set on preformed piers with metal post anchors.

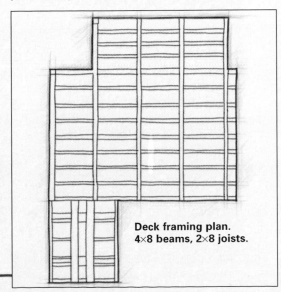

Deck framing plan. 4×8 beams, 2×8 joists.

PLANNING FOR SITE PREPARATION

Extensive site preparation is expensive and can sabotage your landscape budget. It involves planning for preservation and demolition, as well as for grading and drainage. You'll want to design your plans to minimize initial site work to save time and money during construction.

PRESERVATION AND DEMOLITION

What you keep and what you get rid of are very important decisions. Protecting everything you want to preserve is the very first thing you should do on site. This crucial step is frequently omitted. There's nothing more distressing than buying a wooded lot because you love the trees only to discover that the contractor has cleared it. Protecting site assets on new lots before houses are built is as important as saving features on existing properties that are being renovated.

Communication is the name of the game. No one working on your property will know what you want to save unless you make it very clear. Don't merely wrap flagging tape around the trees you want to save; your contractor may think that is the signal that you want them removed!

Leave no room for doubt when it comes to cutting down trees.

PROTECTING TREES DURING CONSTRUCTION

Mature trees are an asset and you should protect them from construction damage as much as possible. Temporary barriers will alert contractors to keep heavy equipment and construction debris off tree root areas. Siltation fences can protect trees by preventing displaced soil from building up over their root zone.

Discuss plans with workers to minimize the impact construction has on existing elements. It's not enough to talk to just the general contractor; subcontractors must understand your goals, too. Be certain that signs, flags, or barriers communicate your wishes at a glance. It only takes one worker to make an irreversible or costly mistake.

TIPS FOR TREES

Here's how to protect trees you wish to preserve: Stake the perimeter of the area beneath each tree canopy and enclose the entire area with flagging tape to keep it clear. Flag each tree, writing KEEP on each flag using a bold, black permanent marker.

Demolition should be carefully controlled. Meet with tree cutters to discuss felling strategies. Always move your car and your neighbors', just to be safe. Ask anyone doing work on your property to provide proof of bonding. Otherwise, your homeowners insurance may have to pay for any damage.

When doing earth work, take care to avoid disturbing soil around trees you want to preserve. Exposing roots can dehydrate a tree and invite insect problems. Adding soil on top of the existing surface can kill a tree by suffocating feeder roots. A common construction mistake is allowing heavy equipment or cars to drive or park beneath trees. Stockpiling material near a tree trunk is a bad idea, too. Anything that compacts the soil can potentially kill a tree. Chemicals should never be dumped on site. Don't be naive; contractors may not consider the long-term health of your trees.

SAFETY FIRST

Be aware that you may be liable for anyone injured on your property, including workers and even trespassers. Insist on good safety practices and proper protective gear. Secure the job site to prevent injuries to both invited and uninvited guests. Construction areas are appealing to children; require workers to remove all tools and hazardous materials when they leave each day. Holes should be barricaded; swimming pools should not be filled with water until fences, gates, latches, and life-saving equipment are in place.

COST CONCERNS

Demolition and disposal can become hidden costs that drive a project over budget. Get estimates for demolition before work begins. In addition to labor and equipment expenses, permits, hauling, and dump fees can be

LIMIT ACCESS

Designate and clearly mark a construction entrance for contractors. Place barriers across existing paving to prevent heavy equipment from cracking hard surfaces. If there's no way to avoid driving across an underground sprinkler system, cap one zone and remove the heads to minimize damage. Limit equipment in the protected zone. Though pipe breaks may be unavoidable, leaks will not occur if the zone has been disconnected from the system.

unpleasant surprises. Know what you're getting into from the beginning. Ask contractors to itemize their costs to see if there's any work you can do. If you have a truck, removing debris yourself can be a good way to save money. Make sure your local dump will accept construction rubble and that it is open during your free hours. Recycle what you can.

If there is a complicated strategy for making your new design work with existing site elements, consider producing a site preparation plan. Trace a copy of your master plan and use color codes and labels to convey your intentions. Identify trees and features that remain and those that should be removed. Mark construction access routes and storage areas on your plan and give it to your contractor as soon as he or she arrives on site.

When you obtain an estimate for tree removal, ask if the price includes grinding the stump. Burying stumps can cause fungal problems later.

Raised beds can solve both grading and drainage problems and provide rich soil for plants.

RETAINING WALLS

Retaining walls enable you to radically change your topography. Here, a wall retains a cut in a slope and allows leveling of the area at its base.

Retaining walls allow you to terrace a site creating a level area from a hill with a cut into the slope. Retaining walls can also add height to a flat area by building up soil behind the wall. Stone, brick, concrete, concrete block, or wood treated for ground contact can be used for building retaining walls. Ground water pressure can build up and cause a wall to lean and finally overturn. Small holes, called weep holes, penetrate wall faces to allow water from the soil side to seep through. French drains—perforated pipe centered in a gravel bed—at the back foot of the wall can help alleviate water pressure, but weep holes are still needed. Supports that extend behind the wall into the soil, known as dead men, are needed for tall or wooden walls. Proper footings are also important to keep retaining walls upright.

GRADING

Grading is nothing more than moving earth. You will need to grade your property if you are changing the shape of your land in any way. Creating level areas for play spaces, patios, or walkways requires grading. So will cutting into slopes with retaining walls or adding soil to contribute interest to a flat site.

Mounded soil—known as berms—can give shrubs and trees planted for privacy a head start by making them seem taller right away. Terracing can tame a steep site. Different levels can create distinctions between outdoor rooms within your landscape.

You will make your grading design after you design your hardscape so that the earth work can conform to construction. However, it's a good idea to keep grading in mind while designing both hardscape and planting schemes. A patio proposed on slope will cost more to build than one designed for a naturally level area. If you really want a seating area in that particular spot, consider building a deck instead. Think about the natural characteristics of your site as you plan.

GRADING ORDER

The actual work is done in the reverse order from planning: Rough grading is completed before hardscape projects begin. Finish grades—usually accomplished by hand-raking the surface of the soil—may be set as late as the bed preparation phase of work, just before planting begins. Rough grading may or may not involve large equipment. If there are several contractors on the job, make sure you know that one has included finish grading in his price, or you could get stuck with an unplanned expense. Often, the landscape contractor will plan to do some grading by hand but expects that the general contractor will leave rough grades fairly accurate.

CUT AND FILL

Minimizing the amount of earth that must be cut from slopes or moved to fill low areas will save money and disturb fewer existing plants. If you need to do this type of work, try to remove the same amount of soil needed elsewhere on site. Known as balancing cut and fill, this strategy saves money: You'll avoid hauling expenses to remove soil as well as the cost of buying fill dirt.

At the end of this chapter, you will prepare a conceptual or detailed plan to direct grading and drainage for your new landscape.

You can measure changes in elevation with a string, a level, and a tape measure. Tie a string tightly from a high point to a tall stake driven at a lower point in your yard. Check the string for level with a line level or carpenter's level. Then tie flags (cloth scraps) at equal length along the line (every 5 or 10 feet, for example). At each flag, measure the distance from the line to the ground, keeping the tape measure plumb. Measure in sections if the elevation falls off rapidly over a long distance.

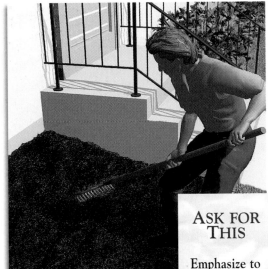

ASK FOR THIS

Emphasize to anyone working on your property that you want positive drainage. This means that you expect paving and earth work to slope enough to move water away from structures and prevent standing water.

WHEN TO HIRE A PRO

There often comes a point in a project when you must decide whether you can accomplish a task yourself or need to hire an expert to help. It's tempting to base this decision solely on the cost of hiring the contractor, but there are other expenditures to consider as well. Your time is valuable. If a grading project will require four weekends of hard labor, you may decide that spending up to $500 to hire someone to do the job on a single Saturday would be money well spent. You'll get things going faster and be able to move on to tasks you are better equipped to perform yourself.

Craftsmen can also contribute a level of skill that may be beyond your abilities. If you have limited experience, skilled carpenters and masons may build portions of your hardscape more neatly than you can. You may save yourself frustration as well as the expense of buying additional materials required by starting over. Study your master plan and question what you can realistically do yourself.

Calling in a professional to help with more intricate parts of the job can be a wise decision that improves the look of your project and can save you time now and money in the long run.

SLEEVES

After grading is done, don't forget to lay conduit beneath areas that will be paved. These empty pipes make it easy to accommodate wires or small pipe that must cross though a hardscape area. Two-inch schedule 40 PVC usually does the job. Lay a few beneath each area that will be paved. Conduit should be laid perpendicular to paving so that pipe reaches from one side to another. The location of sleeves isn't critical; just make sure you've got a way to thread wire beneath paved areas without the expense of boring a passageway. Sleeves will come in handy if you want to add lighting or security systems in the future.

EARTHMOVERS

Large grading projects require earthmoving equipment such as bobcats and front-end loaders. Their expense is usually calculated by the hour, combining an equipment fee with operator's expense, so try to have as much grading done at one time as possible. It is necessary to consider access to your property for such equipment. A temporary construction entrance is often a good idea to prevent cracking caused by driving machinery across existing paving or planting areas.

DRAINAGE

Where is the water going to go? This important question should be asked before the first hole is dug or the first brick is laid.

Standing water can cause patios, driveways, and walks to become slick with mud or moss. Even shallow puddles can become breeding sites for mosquitoes. Wood that stays damp will eventually rot. Rapidly flowing water can wash away plants and mulch, and cause erosion. Poor dispersal of rainwater can drown some plants while leaving others too dry.

RUNOFF

Rain often falls faster than the ground can absorb causing "runoff" water to flow across surfaces. When water finds a level spot, it stays there until it percolates into the soil, evaporates, is absorbed by plants, or is moved by artificial means to a drainage system.

Runoff is increased by water shed from impermeable surfaces such as roofs and paved areas. The less porous a surface, the faster water will flow, and the less likely the ground will absorb it. Whenever possible, return runoff to ground water aquifers by disposing it within the bounds of your property. Runoff that seeps into the soil is following a natural course, which also allows plants to serve as a natural filter. Runoff that is emptied into a storm sewer collects impurities as it flows.

Always direct runoff away from your house and other structures. Water collected near foundations can seep into basements and crawl spaces and cause structural damage. Clay repeatedly wet and dried will expand and contract, causing foundations to shift and floors, walls, and ceilings to crack. Direct

French drains are an uncomplicated way to move water away from foundations, walls, and too-wet planting beds.

PLAN VIEW

Front door

.015

.015

Planting bed

.015

Meet flush

City sidewalk

Even walkways must be angled slightly to move water away. Sheet drainage is the practice of sloping paving to one side to drain runoff into adjacent planting beds. Avoid turning walkways into miniature rivers during hard rains by using sheet drainage instead of directing the flow down the center of the walk.

runoff away from swimming pools to prevent overflow and possible contamination. Raise copings slightly and slope pool decks away from the water's edge. Before you surround your pool deck with paving, think about how you will use the space and consider alternatives—smaller, more intimate seating areas and more planting space near your pool.

DRAINAGE SOLUTIONS

SWALES are small ditches that intercept the flow of water and redirect it around structures. Swales may be planted with grass or lined with concrete or drainage tiles. You can add flexible piping to continue the work of swales beneath features in your yard. Plan where the pipe will daylight—open an end onto the surface of the soil—so you can unobtrusively empty water elsewhere on your lawn. (It is illegal

FRENCH DRAIN SECTION

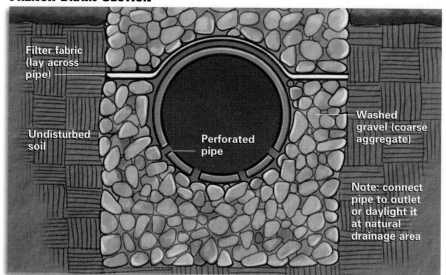

Filter fabric (lay across pipe)

Undisturbed soil

Perforated pipe

Washed gravel (coarse aggregate)

Note: connect pipe to outlet or daylight it at natural drainage area

to alter drainage patterns to increase the flow of runoff onto adjacent properties.) The mat-like characteristic of lawn slows the water down so it can be absorbed into the ground. Dumping runoff into planting beds can wash mulch away and drown plants.

Most swales are inconspicuous. If yours is unsightly, consider decking over it to hide it. Always include a trap door above pipe connections so you can remove debris that may obstruct the flow of water.

CATCH BASINS are underground collection devices. They hold water entering from surface drains and direct it through underground pipes to other destinations, most often storm sewer systems. It is important to set surface drains at the right elevation to capture water. Pipes must slope correctly to move water and connect to existing systems. Underground systems such as those using catch basins should be planned and installed before hardscape is constructed. A landscape architect or civil engineer can assist you with catch basin design, if needed.

FRENCH DRAINS move water in a different manner. Perforated pipe set in a gravel bed can collect excess water and move it away from structures or boggy planting areas. French drains are easy to install yourself. It's a good idea to wrap pipes in filter fabric to keep soil particles from clogging the perforations. Use large, rinsed gravel to fill the trenches.

DETENTION AREAS are artificial depressions made to collect water and hold it temporarily until it can be absorbed into the soil. As concerns about water supplies increase, detention areas are becoming a popular means of handling runoff on-site, instead of allowing it to enter storm sewer systems. This solution is ideal in geographic regions with high rainfall. Detention areas are ideal places to develop moist-soil (or even bog) gardens. See the list at right for some plant suggestions.

TRENCH DRAINS are narrow, prefabricated devices that capture surface water and direct it elsewhere through underground pipes. Unlike catch basins, which resemble underground boxes, trench drains are linear. This makes them great for using at the base of steps or along swimming pool decks.

Drainage can be shown on the same plan as grading. Use small arrows to indicate the direction of flow. A landscape architect can help you design underground systems if your drainage cannot be handled on the surface.

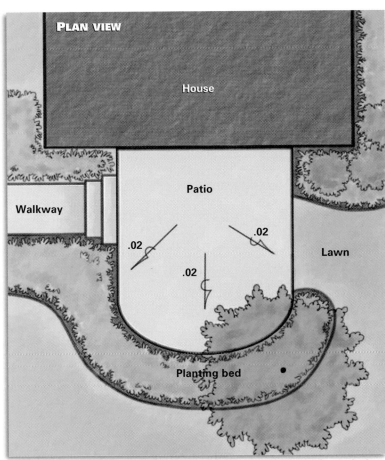

Sloping patios toward their edges eliminates the need for a drain in the center of the paving. Never slope a patio toward your home. A 2 percent slope will move runoff across most paving.

PLANTS FOR MOIST PLACES

HERBACEOUS PERENNIALS
Bee Balm
  (*Monarda didyma*)
Buttercup
  (*Ranunculus* spp.)
Forget-me-not, True
  (*Myosotis scorpiodes*)
Lily, Canada
  (*Lilium canadense*)
Lobelia, Big Blue
  (*Lobelia siphilitica*)
SHRUBS
Arrowwood
  (*Viburnum dentatum*)
Carolina Allspice
  (*Calycanthus floridus*)
Dogwood, Red Osier
  (*Cornus sericea*)
Dogwood, Yellowtwig
  (*Cornus sericea*)
  'Flaviramea'

Inkberry
  (*Ilex glabra*)
Pinkshell Azalea
  (*Rhododendron vasey*)
TREES
Birch, River
  (*Betula nigra*)
Cypress, Bald
  (*Taxodium distichum* var. *distichum*)
Fringetree
  (*Chionanthus virginicus*)
Larch, American
  (*Larix laricina*)
London Plane
  (*Platanus* × *acerifolia*)
Maple, Red
  (*Acer rubrum*)
Oak, Swamp White
  (*Quercus bicolor*)

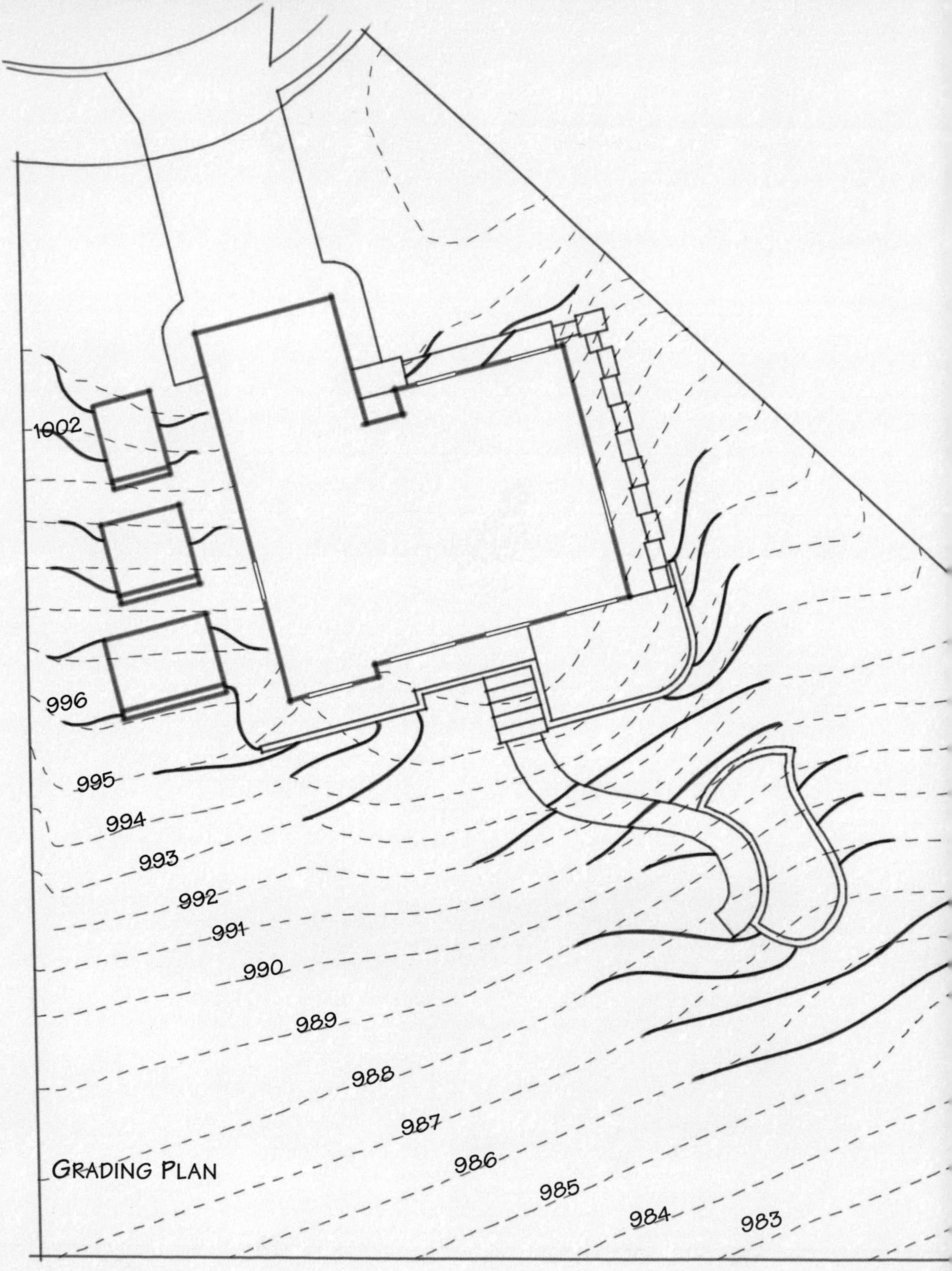

1002

996

995

994

993

992

991

990

989

988

987

GRADING PLAN

986

985

984   983

GRADING AND DRAINAGE PLAN

A grading and drainage plan is a working drawing that shows how earth will be moved to incorporate your design ideas and to move water away from structures. Planning how you will shape the earth also helps you refine your design. If you have a steep site that needs retaining walls, steps, and earth work to create level areas, you'll want to have a grading and drainage plan before the earth-moving equipment arrives.

CONCEPTUAL PLAN

If your site is not steep and grading is uncomplicated, prepare a conceptual grading and drainage plan instead of a detailed working drawing.

Place a tracing of your base map over your layout plan so you can trace new hardscape features. Make notes on this new plan, indicating which areas should be level and which areas you want to raise. Mark inclines, even very slight slopes, with arrows to show the direction storm water will flow. Make sure that water is flowing away from all structures. Paved areas should be sloped to shed water.

TOPOGRAPHY MAP

If you are solving tricky drainage problems or drastically changing the shape of your land, you'll need a detailed grading and drainage plan. Because it is more detailed than a conceptual plan, you will need to have a topography map prepared first.

A topography map shows elevations on your existing terrain. For complex projects, hire a surveyor to shoot elevations and translate the existing form of the earth (refer to the illustration below). Ask if you can have only spot elevations measured or contours shot at 5 foot vertical intervals, instead of 1 foot intervals, to save costs. (The smaller the interval, the longer the survey will take to shoot.) You may only need a portion of the site shot to produce a grading plan that focuses on a specific area if the rest of the site will remain unaltered.

WHAT THE LINES MEAN

On a topography map, the surface of the earth is shown in contour lines, each line representing equal points of elevation. Contour lines are labeled with numbers to show their relationships to each other and to structures on site. The difference between numbers shows the changes in elevation. Contours that appear close together on a plan indicate a steep slope. Those that are far apart represent a level or gradually sloping area.

On a grading and drainage plan, dashed lines show existing contours. Solid lines show how the contours will change with grading. A plan as complex as the sample on the left would likely need to be drawn by a professional. If your plan is equally complex, it's probably a good idea to consult a landscape architect. Bring copies of your master plan and layout plan. They will be the basis for the more detailed working drawing your site requires.

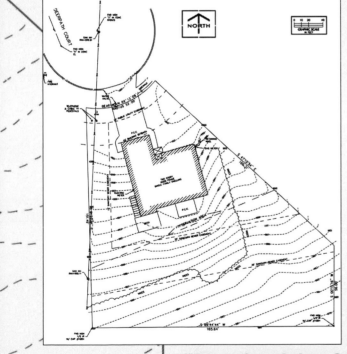

When to Commission a Survey
A topography map shows the existing surface of the earth. A grading and drainage plan shows existing topography as well as changes that will be made to the shape of the earth. A topography map prepared by a surveyor is necessary to produce a detailed grading plan and drainage plan. You won't need a topography map if grading and drainage changes are minimal. You can conceptualize your goals with arrows showing the flow of water and notes about where to add or remove small amounts of soil.

PLANTING DESIGN

The spiky texture of a potted plant placed in a bed makes it the perfect accent to contrast with smooth lawn and water.

EXCITING ACCENTS

Accent is interest achieved through contrast. When the color, texture, line, or form of a plant differs noticeably from the qualities of its setting, the plant stands out. Don't add too many. Plants competing for attention will destroy the unity of your design. Some accents—flowers, fruit, bark, and form—will be seasonal; their contrasts will vary at different times of the year.

SPOTLIGHT WITH FOCAL POINTS

Focal points are fun to add. Nearly anything can be the center of attention. Plants, artwork, gates, and water features make lovely garden highlights. Placement is the key. If your focal point is freestanding, such as a sundial or a small ornamental tree, make sure the background is sufficiently neutral to showcase it. If it's an existing item that you want to spotlight, design the surrounding space to show it off. Aligning new views with existing features will bring energy to the look of your landscape.

DESIGN FUNDAMENTALS

On your master plan you've shown, in a general way, how trees, planting beds, and lawn areas will fit in your new landscape. Now you need more detail—for this, you need a planting plan. As you draw it, you may find you need to alter the bed shapes and tree locations on your master plan, but that's the process of refinement. Your planting plan is also the place you'll add a layer showing shrubs, vines, ground covers, and seasonal color. You'll select specific plants and figure quantities on this plan, too.

Remember, you haven't solved all your problems yet, so refer to your concept diagram and site analysis to refresh your memory about the design problems you want plants to solve. Look for situations where you can apply the following design fundamentals.

This long, fenced driveway could seem unfriendly, but trees framing the entry make it shady and welcoming.

Hedges can form clipped walls of green that add privacy, screen unwanted views, and create an air of formality. If you plan to keep your hedge trimmed, choose an evergreen shrub that does not bear showy flowers.

The low mounding form of this colorful ground cover contrasts with the vertical shape of ornamental grasses, making a simple composition just right for a seaside property where the view beyond is dominant.

FRAMING TECHNIQUES

Framing is another way to play up the best aspects of your home and yard—both new and existing elements. Consider strategic plant arrangements that frame pretty views, decorative items, and architectural attributes. Designers frequently employ framing to call attention to garden entries and to add irresistible allure to the areas beyond them. You can use this technique yourself; first identify the proposed item or area of attention and the angle from which it will be viewed (the sight line). Then position plants so they make a clear path along the sight line. Remember, a sight line can originate from within your home as a view through a window or door to a garden focal point.

PLANT FOR SCREENING

Screening with dense plant groupings is an easy way to block unsightly views and add privacy. These living walls can give an area a sense of intimacy and can also help reduce noise and mitigate harsh winds or glare.

For privacy, plant evergreens or deciduous plants or a combination of the two. Decide which views you need to block to give either interior or exterior rooms (or both) privacy. Next, determine how much privacy you want—total and continuous or partial and seasonal? A single tree may be all you need. Evergreen shrubs are good for total, year-round barriers. Consider screens as backdrops for other plants or accent items.

DELINEATE YOUR SPACE

Plants are also great for giving shape to areas. Design your planting to help create the zones that you identified on your concept diagram (see page 36). Formal hedges, informal shrub groupings, groves of trees, or a single tree properly placed can define space.

Plants do not have to be taller than eye-level to shape space. Even a minor barrier makes one area of the landscape distinct from another. Think about the inside of your home. Walls form the most obvious space dividers, but a waist-high bar may define the kitchen, and furniture groupings may establish zones of conversation within the living room. Plants of varying heights can play similar roles in your outdoor rooms.

Rich textures make this planting scheme interesting, while compatible colors keep the composition harmonious.

EVERGREEN OR DECIDUOUS?

Is the plant you are considering evergreen or deciduous? Find out before you buy. Evergreen plants do not shed their leaves in a single season and provide year-round greenery. Deciduous plants may be leafless for months. Both types of plants add value to your landscape, but make sure you know what to expect, especially when choosing plants for screening views.

TREES

Like other plants, properly placed trees can be used to solve design problems in your landscape. They can become accents, add privacy, define zones of use, make an area seem people-sized, provide shade, and contribute vertical definition. Like no other plant, trees can prevent the landscape (especially new-home lots) from looking flat and static.

Design should influence your choices. For each location on your master plan, list the characteristics of the ideal tree. For example, a tree for the center of an entry courtyard should be relatively small when mature, have noninvasive roots that won't buckle paving, have accent qualities at least part of the year and remain attractive even when not in peak color. A green Japanese maple (*Acer palmatum*) fits the bill, slowly growing to a mature height of about 20 feet. Its lacy foliage is attractive in spring and summer and becomes bright red in fall. The sculptural form of its trunk, branches, and fine twigs makes it wonderfully interesting in the dead of winter.

When listing characteristics to match your design needs, note what won't work, as well. For example, you won't want damaging roots near concrete, messy fruit near sitting or parking areas, or tall trees beneath power lines or eaves.

By writing descriptions, it will be easy to pick the right one for the right spot. Even if you don't know anything about plants, you can get the information you need from nurseries (bring your master plan and list of corresponding descriptions). Local nurserymen, landscape architects, garden designers, and extension agents can help you with the selection process. You'll also want to choose trees that thrive in your climate zone, and you'll need to know something about their cultural characteristics, too—which trees grow in sun or shade and which trees require good drainage or boggy soil. Make notes of the trees on your list. You will need to specify your trees by name when you produce your planting plan.

If you can't afford to do anything else, plant trees. Tree prices depend on availability, size, difficulty of delivery, rate of growth, and packaging. Buy them small and watch them grow. You will get more long-term value from even a tiny, young tree than you will from a flat of annuals. A house sitting on its lot is just a house, but a house nestled within trees is a home.

Container-grown trees may cost more but adjust to new locations quickly.

Balled-and-burlapped trees cost less and may decline initially upon planting but usually grow well after an adjustment period.

CHECKLIST FOR CHOOSING TREES

Here are the characteristics you should use in evaluating trees for your planting plan.

- Purpose of tree within your design
- Mature size (height and spread); rate of growth
- Evergreen or deciduous
- Seasonal interest
- Form
- Cultural requirements
- Availability and expense
- Negative characteristics to avoid

CONTAINER-GROWN OR BALLED-AND-BURLAPPED?

Except for fruit trees, which may be sold bare-root, most trees are sold in containers or with their rootballs wrapped in fabric (balled-and-burlapped). Small container-grown trees are reasonably priced. They start their lives in containers, not in fields, so their roots are never disturbed by digging, and they grow readily after planting. Make sure the container soil isn't loose and crumbly; it may mean that a tree with small roots has been placed in a larger container.

Balled-and-burlapped trees (sometimes called B&B) are dug from fields and may suffer transplant shock upon planting. Keep them watered, even if all the leaves drop. After the tree adjusts to its environment, new leaves will appear. Larger balled-and-burlapped trees and shrubs can be purchased at a lower cost than large container-grown plants. Always inspect rootballs for damage before purchasing. A tree with a large rootball and short height is a better investment than a tall, spindly tree with a puny rootball. The bigger rootball gives the tree a better chance of survival and quicker means of becoming established.

CHART OF DECIDUOUS TREES

Common/botanical name	Height/Spread at Maturity	Moisture Conditions	Growth Rate	Zone	Benefits
Cimarron ash (*Fraxinus pennsylvanica* 'Cimarron')	55'/25'	moderate–dry	moderate	3–7	wildlife, fall color
Bald cypress (*Taxodium distichum*)	150'/40'	moist	moderate	3–10	wildlife, fall color
Carolina buckthorn (*Rhamnus carolinianus*)	25'/15'	moist	slow	6–9	wildlife, fall color, fruit
Paper birch (*Betula papyrifera*)	40'/30'	moderate	fast	3–4	bark
River birch (*Betula nigra*)	100'/45'	moist	moderate	4–9	bark
Southern catalpa (*Catalpa bignonioides*)	25'/30'	moderate	moderate	5–7	blooms, form
Narrow–leaf cottonwood (*Populus angustifolia*)	45'/25'	moderate–dry	moderate	3–8	wildlife, foliage
Kousa dogwood (*Cornus kousa*)	20'/25'	moist	moderate	5–8	flower, fall color
Chinese elm (*Ulmus parvifolia*)	50'/35'	all	rapid	6–9	fall color, bark
Crape myrtle (*Lagerstroemia indica*)	25'/25'	moderate	moderate	7–9	flowers, wildlife
Goldenrain tree (*Koelreuteria paniculata*)	25'/25'	moderate	moderate	5–9	flower, fruit
Honeylocust (*Gleditsia triacanthos*)	50'/30'	moderate	moderate	3–9	wildlife, form
Littleleaf linden (*Tilia cordata*)	65'/40'+	moderate	moderate	3–6	wildlife, form
Sugar maple (*Acer saccharum*)	75'/50'	moderate	moderate	4–7	wildlife, fall foliage
Red maple (*Acer rubrum*)	120'/50'	moist	moderate	3–9	wildlife, red fall color
Bur oak (*Quercus macrocarpa*)	50'/50'	moderate	moderate	3–8	foliage
Pin oak (*Quercus palustris*)	60'/40'	average, acidic	fast	5–8	shade, rapid effect
Russian olive (*Elaeagnus angustifolia*)	25'/25'	moderate–dry	moderate	3–7	wildlife, yellow blooms
Callery pear (*Pyrus calleryana*)	25'/25'	moderate	moderate	5–9	flower, fall color
Thundercloud plum (*Prunus cerasifera* 'Thundercloud')	25'/20'	moderate	moderate	4–6	flower, foliage
Texas mesquite (*Prosopis glandulosa*)	25'/25'	dry	slow	9–11	flower, wildlife
Eastern redbud (*Cercis canadensis*)	25'/25'	moderate	moderate	5–7	flower, foliage
Tulip tree (*Liriodendron tulipifera*)	120'/50'	moist	rapid	5–7	very large, rapid effect

CHART OF EVERGREENS

Common/Botanical Name	Height/Spread at Maturity	Moisture Conditions	Growth Rate	Zone	Benefits
White fir (*Abies concolor*)	40'/30'	moderate	moderate	5–7	foliage
Leyland cypress (× *Cupressocyparis leylandii*)	50'/20'	moderate	rapid	5–7	pest free
Southern live oak (*Quercus virginiana*)	50'/50'	dry	moderate		wildlife, form
Austrian pine (*Pinus nigra*)	50'/30'	moderate–dry	moderate	4–6	roadway, screening, good specimen
White pine (*Pinus strobus*)	70'/35'	moderate	rapid	3–9	screening
Colorado blue spruce (*Picea pungens glauca*)	75'/35'	moderate	slow	3–7	good specimen
Norway spruce (*Picea abies*)	60'/30'	moderate	rapid	3–7	screening

SHRUBS

You can give your yard shape, style, presence, and privacy by adding shrubs. Consider them for accents, too. Many shrubs flower and fruit at different times of the year and are good seasonal show-offs. Shrubs range in size from dwarf and pygmy selections to plants the size of small trees.

Azaleas add a trail of color leading to a traditional home, in an example of seasonal accent.

PRIORITIZE YOUR PLANTING

When you're preparing your planting plan, prioritize your shrub planting: Which design problems do you need to solve first? Compare your site analysis with your master plan. You probably haven't solved all the problems yet. Look for places where you want to add privacy or improve the view of your home from the street. You may want to plant these areas first, especially front-yard foundations—they influence the appearance of your home.

You'll want to plant trees before your shrubs because their locations are slightly more critical. You also need room to maneuver when planting trees; adding shrubs after trees keeps these smaller plants from getting stepped on.

Foundation planting refers to plants set near the base of a house. They hide foundations and marry the architecture with the land. To be effective, foundation plantings should be more than mere rows of shrubs. Consider filling beds in tiers or layers to give shape to the landscape and to provide a transition from the vertical form of the house to the horizontal lawn. Shrubs are effective in such mass plantings, and you can complement them with small trees, vines, perennials, ground covers, and annuals.

The most common mistake made with foundation planting is underestimating mature sizes. If a shrub will require lots of pruning in the future to prevent it from blocking a window or crowding a walkway, then it is not the right choice for that location. Know how high and wide a shrub will grow before digging a hole for it. And resist the temptation to plant shrubs too closely together; you'll avoid future maintenance headaches.

MATCH SHAPE TO LOCATION

Understanding what shape plants will eventually assume will prevent you from making another foundation planting error—choosing the wrong form for the location. Pick shrubs that match your expectations. If you want a tailored look near the house, for example, don't use informal plants such as Border forsythia (*Forsythia intermedia*). Its graceful, arching form is easily ruined by excessive pruning. Plan ahead to display the plant's natural shape within a foundation composition. If it does not fit the look you're after, plant it elsewhere in the yard or omit it altogether. Select a more compact, geometrically-shaped shrub instead, such as Common boxwood (*Buxus sempervirens*) if your foundation planting scheme is formal.

CHART OF SCREENING SHRUBS

Common/Botanical Name	Height/Spread at Maturity	Moisture Conditions	Growth Rate	Zone	Benefits
Arborvitae, 'Emerald Giant' (*Thuja* 'Emerald Green')	20'/6'	moderate	fast	3–7	upright, narrow
Oriental arborvitae (*Thuja orientalis* 'Aurea Nana')	5'/2.5'	moderate	moderate	3–9	compact form
Heavenly bamboo (*Nandina domestica*)	8'/8'	moderate	moderate	6–9	wildlife
Northern bayberry (*Myrica pensylvanica*)	12'/12'	moderate	moderate	3–6	fragrant
Japanese camellia (*Camellia japonica*)	15'/10'	wet	slow	7–9	flowers
Carolina cherrylaurel (*Prunus caroliniana*)	25'/20'	moderate	moderate	7–10	flowers
Pathfinder juniper (*Juniperus scopularum* 'Pathfinder')	15'/5'	moderate	moderate	4–8	very narrow form
American holly (*Ilex opaca*)	20'/8'	moderate	slow	5–9	wildlife, cuttings

SCREEN AND SHAPE

Shrubs can also screen. Evergreen shrubs offer year-round privacy and are best for blocking unsightly items such as garbage cans or utility boxes. Tall shrubs can block views looking into your property and make outdoor living areas more enjoyable.

Avoid shrubs with dense forms when planning for areas that need good air circulation—you don't want to block the air from your air conditioner, for example. Choose open-structured shrubs instead or substitute lattice panels.

You can use shrubs, of course, to define zones of use within your landscape. Shrub beds can transform a boring run-on lawn into charming garden rooms. A bed of moderate sized shrubs may also be the ticket for separating a play area from a patio. Parents can watch the children play and still enjoy their own conversation area.

CUTTING UP

Before you cut down an overgrown shrub, consider the possibility of pruning it to resemble a small tree. You'll save the cost of removal and replacement. To transform a shrub into a tree form, cut off the lower branches to reveal the trunk. Avoid a lollipop look by leaving several main branches or multiple trunks. Stand back and check your progress frequently. Trim stray branches as needed but resist the urge to radically alter the canopy shape.

As you did for trees, list the qualities your shrubs will need to meet the needs you've shown on your master plan. Research which shrubs thrive in your climate and conditions of your landscape. You'll list the species by name on the plan and draw them to scale. Then you can determine quantities, estimate costs, and make shopping lists.

The play of textures and foliage colors in this planting bed is set off by a sweep of lawn, giving this ordinary home eye-catching curb appeal.

A dynamic, rectilinear line formed by a clipped hedge separates a parking area in the background from the rest of the garden.

CHART OF FOUNDATION SHRUBS

Common/Botanical name	Height/Spread at Maturity	Light Conditions	Growth Rate	Zone	Benefits
Azalea (many varieties)	6'/6'	moderate	slow	5–9	flowers
English yew (*Taxus baccata* 'Repandens')	4'/12'	moderate	moderate	6–7	wide, spreading
Crimson pygmy barberry (*Berberis thunbergii*)	2'/3'	full sun	moderate	4–8	crimson color
Burkwood daphne (*Daphne × burkwoodii*)	4'/4'	shade	slow	4–7	fragrant flowers
Japanese spirea (*Spiraea japonica*)	3'/3'	full sun	rapid	4–8	flowers, fall foliage
Gardenia (*Gardenia jasminoides*)	5'/5'	partial sun	moderate	8–11	fragrant flowers
Guava (*Feijoa sellowiana*)	6'/10'	full sun	moderate	8–11	edible fruit
Japanese holly (*Ilex crenata*)	5'/5'	partial sun	moderate	6–9	compact, foliage
Rhododendron (many varieties)	4'/4'	partial shade	moderate	5–9	flowers

LAWNS AND GROUND COVERS

Defining the edges is what separates mere grass from a gracious lawn. This carpet of green stands out because it is framed by flowers and hedges.

Lawns and ground covers, along with hardscape, make the floors of your outdoor rooms. Lawns are the most durable of plantings, making them an excellent choice for play areas. Lawns can be grand and sweeping or tiny and sculpted. But no matter what style or size they are, lawns are more than level surfaces for play. With proper planning, lawns can tie the landscape together.

So, too, can ground covers, plants that hug the earth. Some are grass-like; others are creeping vines. Still more are spreading plants. Although they have uses similar to lawns, and can be used as a lawn companion, ground covers, in general, produce a less tailored look. Lawns and ground covers present you with still another opportunity to design with color, texture, line, and form.

SHAPE WITH BED LINES

The best thing you can do for your lawn is to give it a definite shape. When sketching ideas for your planting plan, pay close attention to the bed line—it shapes both the planting beds and lawn areas, and that makes it critical to your plan. You can use bed lines to give form to your ideas and to balance the mass of plants against the empty spaces.

Contrasting plant colors, textures, and heights will call attention to the bed line, highlighting the bed and lawn shapes. In its simplest form, the bed line may be nothing but a shovel-cut edge to keep lawn and ground cover from growing together. It may also be as elaborate as a mortared brick mow strip.

Bed lines can follow any shape you want. Generous, flowing curves will give your landscape a natural look and soften angular lines of architecture. (Avoid fussy lines with lots of little curves; the lawn will lose its shape and the complicated edge will be difficult to maintain.) A square panel of lawn (or any symmetrical shape) will look quite formal. Straight lines can melt into curves, or combine corners and curves to create unusual shapes, but remember—keep it simple.

SOLVING OTHER PROBLEMS

When a bed line crosses a walkway, make sure the lines on both sides match, as if the line were drawn across the walk. Intersect the walk at right angles so you won't form angles which are difficult to mow. If you're using ground cover, repeat the plants in beds on both sides of the walk to give the impression that a person on the path is walking through the landscape instead of walking beside it.

Some ground cover species thrive in shade where grass refuses to grow. Ground cover is also great for solving both design and maintenance problems in areas that are difficult to mow, such as steep slopes or around tree roots. Or omit grass altogether and use ground cover as the lowest surface of your planting design. Because you won't be mowing this area, add a thick mulch layer or rake preemergent herbicide into the soil before planting to prevent weed germination.

Many kinds of ground covers will thrive in shady areas where grass won't grow. Check plant tags for adaptability to low light. Wildflowers and lady fern flourish in this meadow glen.

STARTING NEW LAWNS

SODDING

Because you can trim sod to follow bed lines, it will help shape your landscape. It is, however, considerably more expensive than seed.

Lay sod as soon as it's delivered so the roots won't dry out. Set each roll firmly against the previous one, staggering the end joints. During hot weather, water daily, soaking through to the soil beneath.

SEEDING

Seeding costs less (60 to 70 percent less) but demands patience. Use a drop spreader, making two passes at right angles. Rake seeds into the soil and mulch. Keep the birds away and the weeds out, and keep soil evenly moist while seeds are germinating and when seedlings appear. Water regularly until the lawn is thick and full.

HOW GRASSES MEASURE UP

Grasses	Heat Tolerance	Cold Tolerance	Drought Tolerance	Shade Tolerance	Wearability	Low Mowing	Fertilizer Needs	How to Start
COOL-SEASON								
Creeping bentgrass	poor	good	poor	moderate	poor	good	high	seed
Kentucky bluegrass	moderate	good	moderate	moderate	moderate	moderate	moderate	seed
Rough bluegrass	poor	good	poor	good	moderate	moderate	moderate	seed
Canada bluegrass	poor	good	moderate	moderate	poor	poor	low	seed
Fine fescues	moderate	good	moderate	good	good	poor	moderate	seed
Perennial ryegrass	moderate	moderate	moderate	moderate	good	moderate	moderate	seed
Tall fescues	good	poor	good	moderate	good	poor	moderate	seed
WARM-SEASON								
Bahiagrass	good	poor	moderate	moderate	good	poor	low	seed, sprigs, or sod
Hybrid bermudagrass	good	moderate	good	poor	good	good	moderate	sprigs
Blue gramagrass	good	moderate	good	poor	poor	moderate	low	seed
Buffalograss	good	good	good	poor	moderate	good	good	seed or plugs
Carpetgrass	high	poor	moderate	poor	poor	good	low	seed or sprigs
Centipedegrass	good	poor	moderate	moderate	poor	moderate	moderate	seed, sprigs, or plugs
St. Augustinegrass	good	poor	poor	good	moderate	poor	moderate	plugs
Zoysiagrass	good	moderate	good	moderate	good	good	low	seed or plugs

CHART OF GROUND COVERS

Common/botanical name	Zone	Light	Comments
Bergenia (*Bergenia cordifolia*)	4–8	shade or sun	pink flowers, bold evergreen leaves
Bugleweed (*Ajuga*)	4–8	sun–partial shade	pink, blue or purple flowers
Bloody cranesbill (*Geranium sanguineum*)	3–8	sun–partial shade	magenta flowers, red fall foliage
Winter creeper euonymus (*Euonymus fortunei*)	5–8	shade	evergreen foliage
Lily turf (*Liriope*)	6–10	light shade	evergreen
Pachysandra (*Pachysandra terminalis*)	3–7	light shade	evergreen; very resilient
Creeping Thyme (*Thymus serpyllum*)	5–7	sun	fragrant foliage
Vinca (*Vinca minor*)	3–7	shade	evergreen; blue spring flowers

FLOWER BEDS

Growing flowers is one of gardening's joyous rewards. Plan ahead to include locations in your landscape for seasonal color. Soil high in organic matter with good drainage and sites with adequate sun make foolproof flower beds.

ANNUALS AND PERENNIALS

Annuals are colorful bedding plants that may bloom through a season or two but will die before the year is over. Perennials come back year after year. Both add sparkle to your landscape. There are annuals and perennials for sun, for shade, and plants that will thrive in between, so get to know conditions in your yard before you make selections.

Some flowers, such as perennial daylilies, are planted for their blossoms. Others, such as hostas, are known more for their foliage. But don't overdo your color choices; you can kill a good design with a hodge podge of color.

To get the most impact for your money, consider a single flower color. Even one flat of solid-color annuals—yellow pansies, for example—can do a lot to dress up your yard. Plant a thick patch in a highly visible place. Save a handful of plants to grow in containers and set them near your flower bed. A simple scheme will be bright and eye-catching.

TEMPORARY COLOR

Annuals live for less than a year. Perennials reappear season after season. However, a perennial in a mild climate may live for only one season in a harsh climate, so the terms are relative. Many tropical plants that grow year-round in Florida or Southern California can be used to highlight summer gardens elsewhere. Though they won't survive the frost, these bright, fast-growing plants will give your landscape a temporary burst of color and add to your enjoyment.

Count on flowers to welcome you home. Design your landscape with seasonal color in mind, and reserve strategic spots for flowers. Examine your master plan and concept diagram; look for potential accent areas and focal points and decide which views are important.

Plant color with a purpose. Plan now, not only for the color, but for their background and for the seasons, too. Then you can make specific choices on your planting plan.

CHART OF ANNUALS

Common/Botanical Name	Height	Color	Light	Comments
Alyssum (*Lobularia maritima*)	5"	white, blue, pink	sun	compact
Ageratum (*Ageratum houstonianum*)	4–12"	blue	sun	appears as a blue haze
Bachelor button (*Centaurea cyanus*)	18–36"	blue, pink, red, white	sun	re-seeds itself
Baby blue-eyes (*Nemophila menziesii*)	6–8"	blue with white centers	sun	well suited to rock gardens
Joseph's coat (*Amaranthus tricolor*)	3'	red/orange	sun	dry areas
Begonia (*Begonia semperflorens-cultorum*)	6–12"	mixed	sun	container and garden
Cosmos (*Cosmos bipinnatus*)	3'	red–yellow	sun	great show
Globe amaranth (*Gomphrena globosa*)	10–24"	red white		good for cutting
Impatiens (*Impatiens* hybrids)	5–14"	all except blue	partial shade	all-summer bloom
Marigold (*Tagetes*)	12–36"	yellow–orange	sun	beds, borders, containers
Annual Phlox (*Phlox drummondii*)	12–18"	red, purple, white	sun	great bedding plant
Petunia (*Petunia*)	12–18"	all colors	sun	bedding, containers

Single-color schemes make even a small bed turn heads. Here, light pink petals complement the paving.

Hanging baskets are an excellent way to elevate color above ground level.

Think about adding flowers near the front door or at a garden entry. Surround a focal point or plant them at the end of a path. Mix different colors and textures in layered borders for a colorful, cottage-style appearance. Plant taller plants in the back where they won't overshadow their shorter companions. Try sprinkling a unifying color throughout your composition.

Flowers show off best when planted in conjunction with something solid and neutral. A bed of evergreen shrubs or ground cover, a wall or fence, or even the foot of a bench can provide an excellent background for flowers.

You may want to incorporate flowers, especially perennials, into the landscape as a companion for shrubs and ground covers. Remember, perennials have a dormant season, usually winter, so make sure your composition can carry on without looking barren until perennials reappear. Evergreen shrubs and

When planting a mixture of flower colors and forms, frame them with a solid wall, neat fence, or plain, green lawn. This will keep the composition balanced instead of becoming messy and overwhelming.

ground cover planted near perennials provide bright blooms and foliage—a neutral background that shows colors to their best advantage. When the perennials disappear during dormancy, the evergreen plants keep the landscape from appearing empty.

CHART OF PERENNIALS

Common/Botanical Name	Height	Color	Light	Zone
Yarrow (*Achillea*)	18"	yellow, red, and others	full sun	3–8
Lily of the Nile (*Agapanthas*)	4'	deep blue	sun	8–10
Peruvian lily (*Alstroemeria*)	3'	red	partial shade	7–10
Aster (*Aster*)	1–4'	blue	sun	4–8
Mums (*Chrysanthemum*)	1–3'	yellow, bronze, red	sun	4–8
Coreopsis (*Coreopsis*)	6–24"	yellow w/brown centers	sun	6–10
Crocus (*Crocus*)	2–6"	purple, white, and others	sun	2–8
Pinks (*Dianthus*)	6"	blue, rose	sun	2–10
Blanket flower (*Gallardia*)	2–4'	red, yellow, and others	sun	5–9
Daylily (*Hemerocallis*)	6"–5'	yellow, orange, combos	sun	3–9
Rose mallow (*Hibiscus moscheutos*)	6'	pink, purple, white	sun	5–9
Plantain lily (*Hosta*)	6–18"	blue, white, but grown for foliage	shade	4–8
Red hot poker (*Kniphofia*)	6'	red and yellow	sun	6–9
Blazing star (*Liatris*)	4'	purple	sun	5–9

Espalier is an old technique that enables you to grow plants in tight places. Because fruit trees need regular pruning, they are good choices for espalier.

Raised beds are good for growing lots of produce in a small space. This method also makes it easy to add rich soil, improve drainage, and means less bending for the gardener.

Edible plants have many ornamental qualities as well. Plant squash, thyme, and smoky fennel for color and texture as well as for tasty harvests.

EDIBLE ADDITIONS

Let your landscape contribute to your kitchen. Add edible plants to your yard and discover the satisfaction that even the smallest of harvests can bring.

Find room for fruit, vegetables, nuts, or herbs in your plans. Check your site analysis for open, sunny areas and compare them with the uses you planned on your concept diagram. There may be a way to include edible additions in your master plan.

Combine herb or vegetable plots with flowers for a charming kitchen garden. Plenty of sun, a convenient source of water, and good drainage are the main requirements. Locate it for convenient tending and harvesting—just outside the kitchen door.

Many edible plants can be ornamental, too. A fruit tree makes a lovely espalier (a plant that is trained to grow flat against a wall or trellis). This pretty look also yields a harvest. Consider apple, pear, and cherry trees— they respond well to such pruning.

Plants that produce fruit can also solve specific design problems. Blueberry and gooseberry bushes grow large enough to make deciduous screens. The large leaves of figs add coarse texture to any composition. Hickories and Chinese chestnuts contribute shade and nuts. Train hazelnuts to form small trees.

A PLACE FOR EVERYTHING

Some fruits and vegetables can be planted intensely for big yields from small spaces. Though sprawlers such as melons, pumpkins, and squash may not fit in your yard, try carrots, lettuce, cabbage, broccoli, spinach, eggplant, peppers, and onions. Cucumbers and grapes can be trained on trellises; cherry tomatoes and strawberries will produce well in pots. Grow edible flowers such as nasturtiums and violas for a sprinkle of color in salads.

Tuck low-growing plants, such as golden oregano and creeping thyme, into crevices between stepping stones, or include herbs as a facing border for taller plants. The dense green foliage of parsley, for example, makes an excellent foreground for summer caladiums. Rosemary and Spanish lavender can be pruned into single-stem topiaries called standards that add interest to any setting. Herbs also grow happily in pots, which makes them an excellent choice for patios, steps, and window sills.

20 ORNAMENTAL EDIBLES

SHRUBS
Hardy Kiwi
Guava
Paw-paw
Highbush blueberry
Oriental Persimmon
Red currant
Persian Limes
Chiotto oranges
Highbush cranberries
Gooseberries
Rugosa roses (hips)
Quince

GROUND COVERS
Oregano
Strawberries
Thyme
Ornamental vegetables/herbs
Curly parsley
Red leaf lettuce
Dwarf curly kale
Red swiss chard
Rhubarb

VINES

Vines in a design are the mark of an expert. Don't overlook these wonderful plants. Put yourself in the professional league by including mood-making climbers when you prepare your planting plan.

Plant vines in locations where you need privacy, shade, or vertical interest—or perhaps you need to soften a blank wall or a harsh angle. Vines also lend a sense of maturity to new structures and give an air of romance and nostalgia to whatever they cover. Flowering vines contribute color and fragrance. Like other members of the plant world, vines may be evergreen or deciduous.

PLANT WITH FORETHOUGHT

The two most important things to learn about any vine are its method of climbing and growth rate. The wrong vine in the wrong place can damage structures; match growth to location and you will avoid such problems.

Vines that twine or those with tendrils are unlikely to damage wood. Clematis tangles daintily up and over light poles, trellises, and fences without causing harm. Climbing roses tumble on top of themselves, leaning against whatever is handy. You may have to provide support and encourage twiners to grow on fences or up the sides of garages and sheds.

Annual vines, such as morning glory, moon vine, and sweet peas, can be grown from seed for quick, seasonal displays of foliage and flowers. They are too lightweight to inflict damage. Tropical vines, including yellow allamanda and pink mandevilla, are often sold as annuals in cooler regions; use them for temporary splashes of summer color. Plan

to remove all annual vines after the first frost.

Some vines climb by clinging to structures with adhesive disks. These plants can destroy wood and masonry surfaces that are not in good condition. If removed, they will leave aerial rootlets behind as spider-like reminders of their presence. But these adhesive vines are often grown to cloak well-maintained stone or brick surfaces with foliage. English ivy, Boston ivy, and climbing hydrangea are examples. Their dense leaves suggest an air of maturity and establishment often associated with estate landscapes.

Vines that grow too rapidly can also pose problems. Chinese wisteria and trumpet creeper can develop thick, woody stems that are strong enough to lift a roof and heavy enough to topple a fence if not kept within bounds. Japanese honeysuckle can take over a wooded area, but the red-flowered trumpet honeysuckle makes a tame addition to the landscape and attracts hummingbirds.

A climbing hydrangea vine adds a sheaf of texture to the flat facade of this home, suggesting an estate look.

A rustic arbor, made of just two posts and a crosspiece, is transformed by garlands of climbing roses.

Sweet peas climb by tendrils, and they won't damage wood. These bright bloomers need support to encourage them to climb.

20 RECOMMENDED VINES

Variegated porcelain vine
  (*Ampelopsis brevipedunculata* 'Elegans')
Monkshood vine (*Ampelopsis aconitifolia*)
Trumpet creeper
  (*Campsis radicans*)
Sweet autumn clematis
  (*Clematis paniculata*)
Virgin's bower
  (*Clematis virginiana*)
Lavender trumpet vine
  (*Clytostoma callistegioides*)
Hyacinth bean
  (*Dolichos lablab*)

Variegated ivy, 'Gold Heart'
  (*Hedera* spp., varigated)
Climbing hydrangea
  (*Hydrangea petiolaris*)
Blackie sweet potato vine
  (*Ipomoea batatas*, 'Blackie')
Cypress vine, Cardinal climber, Star glory
  (*Ipomoea quamoclit* or *Ipomoea × multifida*)
Red jasmine
  (*Jasminum beesianum*)
Royal jasmine
  (*Jasminum grandiflorum*)

Hummingbird vine
  (*Manettia cordifolia* var. *glabra*)
Evergreen wisteria
  (*Milletia reticulata*)
Mina lobata
  (*Quamoclit lobata*)
Red passionflower
  (*Passiflora coccinea*)
Pink trumpet vine
  (*Podranea ricasoliana*)
Mexican flame vine
  (*Senecio confusus*)
Potato vine
  (*Solanum jasminoides*)

BED PREPARATION

If your soil quality is poor, consider building the soil up to form a raised bed. As little as 4 to 6 inches of rich soil will support many kinds of annuals. Mound soil slightly so water will drain toward the sides. Frame beds to contain soil. Select framing material to match the shape of your bed.

The best landscape plan will fail without proper soil. It is soil that provides all plants with water and nutrients; soil is what anchors plant roots. The attention you give soil in this planning stage will pay you back with years of healthy plants and lawn.

Few sites are blessed with the "rich, well-drained garden loam" recommended in most planting directions. But you can modify almost any kind of soil to grow the plants in your plan, as long as your climate suits them.

MAKING GOOD SOIL

A good soil for planting has topsoil that is several inches deep, is reasonably fertile, has a good balance of sand, silt, and clay particles, and just the right amount of air space between those particles to promote balanced drainage and water retention.

Good soil must also have acceptable pH— a measure of its acid and alkaline properties. The most accurate way to find out your soil pH is to take samples and have them tested by a laboratory. State agricultural colleges usually do soil testing for a nominal charge; many county extension offices also offer the service. If neither is available in your area, check the yellow pages under laboratories. Or you can also easily test your own soil with an inexpensive kit from a garden center.

SOIL AMENDMENTS

No matter what soil problems you start with, from heavy clay that drains too slowly to light sandy soil that drains too quickly, the best thing you can do is to amend it by adding lots of organic matter. As it decomposes, it creates humus—a soft, dark substance that improves drainage, structure, microbial activity, aeration, and other soil properties. Aged manure, ground bark, and straw are common organic amendments. Agricultural by-products such as peanut hulls, cocoa bean hulls, or ground corncobs are also excellent and inexpensive; check to see what is available in your area. A quick method of amending your soil is to purchase and import topsoil. If your topsoil is shallow, this may be the best solution.

PREPARING BEDS

Some of your landscape plantings will require bed preparation. Determine the size you want these areas to be, and then measure and stake them before preparing the soil. If you would like to create a freeform bed, you can define the shape with a garden hose (see page 78). When preparing the soil for the beds, you can

SOIL PREPARATION FOR LAWNS

You can start a new lawn from seed, sod, sprigs, or plugs. Sod is best for lawns if you're in a hurry; seed is cheaper, less labor-intensive, and offers the greatest choice of turfgrass varieties; plugs are the only choice for some turfgrasses. No matter how you plant, lawns won't grow well unless the soil beneath them is reasonably healthy.

Improving the soil for lawn growth is as important as for any other planting. Take time to test the soil, and be sure to specify that the test is for a lawn. Amend the soil as needed; if your soil doesn't need amending, broadcast a starter fertilizer over the area, about 50 pounds of a 5-10-5 fertilizer per 1,000 square feet.

If your soil is more than 60 percent clay or 70 percent sand, work at least a 2-inch layer of organic matter or a

3-inch layer of rich topsoil into it.

Till to a depth of 6 inches, or on larger lawns, make one or two passes with a tractor-mounted disk. Then broadcast starter fertilizer and rake the surface smooth.

The soil will be soft after this procedure; rent a roller and fill it one-third to one-half full with water and roll the soil. Don't wait long to plant after rolling.

If you are working in an area where an old, undesirable lawn must be removed, rent a sod stripper—a machine about the size of a lawn mower—to take off the existing vegetation. (Consider hiring someone to complete this step.) In either case, be prepared to lose some of your topsoil along with the sod. Then prepare the soil as outlined above.

use the traditional dig-and-till method or the much simpler method of creating raised beds.

DIGGING AND TILLING

Digging and tilling is a traditional option. Turning the soil to the depth of a spade or fork (single digging) is uncomplicated, but labor intensive. First, clean off any debris from the planting area. Spread amendments and fertilizer, and with a shovel, spade, or fork, till them into the soil, turning the soil over to bury the weeds and grass. Dig one row at a time. Forks are effective in light soil; spades work best in clay or uncultivated soil.

To double dig a bed, dig a spade-deep trench about 2 feet wide and cart the soil to the far end of the bed. Now dig the trench another spade depth. If the soil at the bottom of the trench is reasonably good, loosen or turn it with a spade or garden fork to the full depth of the blade or tines, then mix in the amendments thoroughly. If the soil at the bottom is rocky or compacted, remove it, pick out rocks or roots, mix in amendments, and then return it to the trench. Dig the next trench, but turn the topsoil into the previous trench—inverting the layers would bring poorer subsoil to the surface.

If your soil is reasonably fertile and free of rocks and tree roots, rototilling is easier. You can rent a walk-behind rotary tiller at any garden or rental shop. If the soil is hard or dry, it may be necessary to make several passes with the tiller, with each pass tilling a couple of inches deeper than the one before. Make these successive passes at right angles to one another. Do corners by hand.

After tilling, use a cultivator to smooth the surface. For a seedbed with more finely textured soil, use a garden rake. Bury hard clods and rocks below tilling depth at the end of the planting bed.

NO-TILL BED PREPARATION

Here's an easier method for preparing beds for perennials, annuals, and ground covers—even shrubs. It accomplishes all requirements of soil texture, fertility, and pH and requires no tilling. In effect, you're making your own soil. Here's how to build an easy bed right on top of your lawn:

■ Start with a base of sandy loam (purchase it at builders' supply stores), 8 to 12 inches deep. Unless the garden site is extremely weedy, underlying grass need not be removed.

■ Add a thick (6- to 8-inch) layer of compost or aged manure, mounding it smoothly. There is no need to till the beds.

■ Simply prepare each planting hole individually, mixing the loam and compost or manure before placing each new plant.

Dairy manure or compost is a better top dressing and mulch choice than peat, which is extremely difficult to rewet when dry. A thick blanket of manure conserves moisture, helps keep beds weed free, and looks tidy. Over time, earthworms will incorporate the loam and manure, so you'll need to replace it annually.

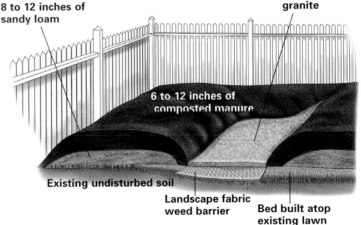

3 to 4 inches of limestone chips or decomposed granite

8 to 12 inches of sandy loam

6 to 12 inches of composted manure

Existing undisturbed soil

Landscape fabric weed barrier

Bed built atop existing lawn

PREPARING BEDS THE EASY WAY

Step 1: Start by laying weed-barrier cloth along the paths. Spread sandy loam 8 to 12 inches deep on top of bed area.

Step 2: Add a 6- to 8-inch layer of compost or aged manure, mounding it smoothly. No need to till.

Step 3: Cover the edges of the weed-barrier cloth with soil, then cover the path with gravel to hold cloth in place.

BASIC PLANTING INSTRUCTIONS

Planting is the task most homeowners are likely to tackle themselves when putting in a new landscape. Although you won't start planting until you're well into landscape construction, it's wise to consider some planting tips ahead of time. The tips will pay off when you put your plans on paper.

BEGIN WITH BED LINES

When your planting plan is completed you'll want to take it outside and replicate the shapes you sketched by laying garden hose to outline the proposed beds. Measure the critical dimensions, approximate the rest, and mark the outlines with lime. Lime is a great way to see outlines of proposed planting areas on the ground before you remove existing grass for new beds. Stake the locations of proposed trees within beds.

Next, you'll remove plants and lawn for bed areas. Transplant only those plants that are healthy, have been pruned correctly, and have new roles in your design. Discard the

rest. As tempting as it is to save everything, you'll waste time and energy preserving stunted and overly pruned plants. Spray grass within proposed beds with a systemic herbicide in hot, sunny weather and wait a few days. Removing dead grass is easier than digging up live lawn.

PLANTING TREES

Plant trees first so you'll have room to maneuver without stepping on other plants. Dig holes twice as wide as rootballs if space allows but only as deep as the rootball. The top of the rootball should be level with the surrounding soil. Digging holes too deep is a common mistake. As soil settles, so does the tree, and the roots may suffocate. If you dig your hole too deep, compact soil at the bottom of the hole to support the rootball.

Stand back (in the place from which you'll view it most often) and examine your tree after placing it in the hole. Turn to present the best face. Mix amendments with native soil to form a half-and-half mixture and fill the hole. Water the soil periodically as you fill. Never tamp soil when planting; small air pockets are part of the soil structure and help transport water to roots. Form a moat of excess soil around the perimeter, mulch inside

TREE PLANTING

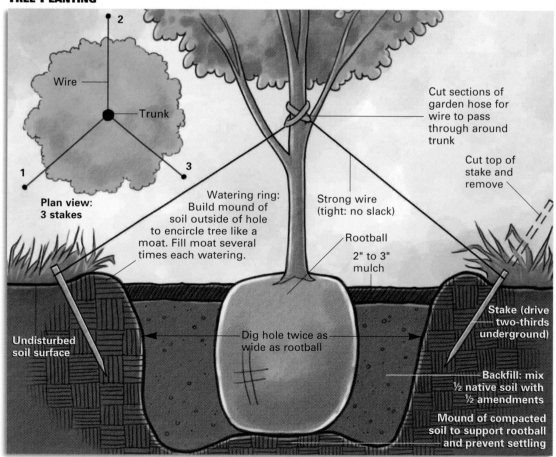

Wire
Trunk

Plan view:
3 stakes

Cut sections of
garden hose for
wire to pass
through around
trunk

Cut top of
stake and
remove

Watering ring:
Build mound of
soil outside of hole
to encircle tree like a
moat. Fill moat several
times each watering.

Strong wire
(tight: no slack)

Rootball

2" to 3"
mulch

Undisturbed
soil surface

Dig hole twice as
wide as rootball

Stake (drive
two-thirds
underground)

Backfill: mix
½ native soil with
½ amendments

Mound of compacted
soil to support rootball
and prevent settling

the ring, and fill the moat slowly with water several times; let it soak in completely. Water daily until new growth appears. In hot weather, new trees may need it twice a day.

SHRUB PLANTING

Shrubs will be next. To get your composition right, set them (still in their containers) throughout the bed before planting the first one. Follow the shape of both your front and rear bed line. Fill middle sections, but don't form recognizable rows. The shrubs will grow together in a mass—forming a shape instead of a line. Space them no closer than two-thirds of their mature spread.

You'll find shrub planting very similar to tree planting. Dig holes wider than they are deep and make sure the rootball is level with the surrounding soil. Mulch around the shrubs but keep the mulch out of stem crotches; they can rot. Use triangular spacing (see illustration on page 81) for setting shrubs, ground covers, perennials, and annuals in beds. Mulch perennial beds well to form an extra winter blanket for roots and bulbs and to keep your beds looking neat. Most perennials should be dug and divided every few years to keep them from overcrowding.

When planting bulbs, prep beds first, then lay bulbs on soil surface. Otherwise, you won't know where you've planted and where you haven't. A bulb auger can make the job easier. Remove annuals from cell packs and position on soil surface before planting.

Always handle plants by the sides of rootballs— never use the stem as a handle. Set plants in holes so the top of the rootball is level with adjacent soil surfaces. If the plant is lower, remove it and fill bottom of hole slightly. Setting plants too low can cause them to drown.

Forming a moat around newly planted trees and shrubs only takes a little extra time but makes a big difference. The ring of soil— which surrounds the hole, not the rootball—helps contain water until it seeps down to roots.

FILLING BEDS

Ground cover, perennial, and annual beds are composed of many small plants. Prepare the entire bed instead of digging single holes. Turn soil over and work in amendments to a depth of 12 to 18 inches. Lay plants or bulbs on top to adjust your composition and spacing. Begin with the front row and work your way back to shape your bed line with plants. Use triangular spacing, staggering the formation and evenly filling the space.

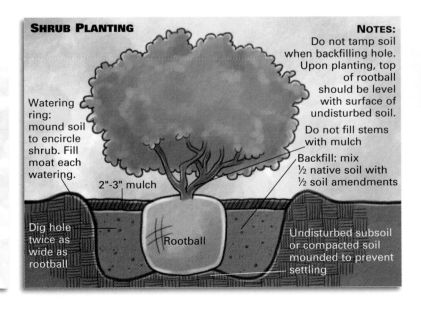

SHRUB PLANTING

NOTES:
Do not tamp soil when backfilling hole. Upon planting, top of rootball should be level with surface of undisturbed soil.

Do not fill stems with mulch

Backfill: mix ½ native soil with ½ soil amendments

Watering ring: mound soil to encircle shrub. Fill moat each watering.

2"-3" mulch

Dig hole twice as wide as rootball

Rootball

Undisturbed subsoil or compacted soil mounded to prevent settling

WHAT'S NEXT

Purchasing plants in the right quantity will make landscaping easier.

There are just a few more things you'll want to know before preparing your own planting plan. Understanding how plants are named, how to select the plants you need, and how to calculate quantities will take a lot of the guesswork out of landscaping.

NOMENCLATURE

Plant names may seem confusing at first. But the system of plant classification and nomenclature is actually designed to eliminate mistakes.

Every plant has a botanical name—its official name. Sometimes called scientific names, these monikers are always Latin. Common names are in plain English, but they're actually more confusing. Several different plants may be called the same thing by different people.

Names proceed from general to specific: the first word is the genus and the second is the species. If a plant is a particular variety or cultivar of a species, it will be noted at the end of the plant name, contained in single quotation marks.

PURCHASE BY BOTANICAL NAME

It's a good idea to specify and purchase plants by their botanical names to make sure you get what you want. Photos in reference materials and plant catalogues can help you recognize plants; they will list both common names and botanical names. Take care to spell botanical names correctly, but don't worry about mangling pronunciation. Just do the best you can.

GETTING STARTED

Choosing the right plants often appears to be a daunting task. You can, of course, hire a landscape architect or garden designer to assist with selection or to produce your planting plan for you. But, with a little research, you will probably find you enjoy doing this stage of design yourself.

Understanding what you need will make decisions easier. Prepare a *planting schematic* to clarify your requirements. Here's how. Lay tracing paper over your master plan. Trace the shapes of trees and beds. Now refer to your concept diagram and site analysis for a reminder of what you want to achieve.

Label planting areas on your tracing paper with descriptions of general qualities that will meet your goals. For example, you may have sketched a mass of plants in a quiet sitting area on your master plan because your concept diagram called for it, but your site analysis also indicates a lack of privacy for that area. Label the plant mass on your planting schematic according to the needs it should fulfill; "screening plants, rapid growers, need to reach 6' to 8' in height, evergreen for year-round privacy, sun-loving."

DESIGN CHARACTERISTICS

Now you've got a starting point. Many plant books contain lists of plants grouped by design characteristics. Find the plants with characteristics similar to the labels on your planting schematic. Decide which plants are worth looking up and use the index to lead you to the sections that contain more information.

If you know the characteristics you are seeking, nurseries can also help you make decisions about what to buy. It's a good idea to visit several nurseries; note their recommendations on your planting schematic before making purchases. (Always ask about mature heights and spreads and recommended spacing between plants, too. These notes will be valuable when you determine quantities of plants needed.)

List several choices for each quality you need. Go ahead and work your favorites into your list of choices, but make sure that design takes precedence over desire. Remember to consider color, texture, and form when you make your final list. You'll be happier in the long run with plants that work together to form an attractive composition. A collection of favorite plants is not always harmonious.

ESTIMATING QUANTITIES

Plant quantities don't have to be a hit-or-miss game. You can get a pretty good idea on paper of what you need to meet your goals.

Figuring quantities for your entire design before digging holes has a couple of advantages. First, you can see whether your plan requires modification to stay within your budget. You may need to trim beds to reduce quantities, but coordinate any reductions with the size and fit of other beds in your plan. It's better to do that on paper than after you've stripped the sod. Saving a little money here and there will not be apparent in the end, but running out of funds before you're finished can make your landscape look awkward.

Second, knowing plant quantities helps determine what you can do now and what you'll do later when time and money permits.

Look up the plants you want to use and note mature sizes on your planting schematic. Double-check the sizes with local gardeners and nurserymen (you'll want local information—plants grow to different sizes in different climates).

SHRUB SPACING

It's important to always keep mature sizes in mind so plants will not outgrow their space. Many shrubs can be spaced at a distance equal to their mature spread. But if growth rates are extremely slow in your locale, plant a little closer than the spacing recommended. If you want to get a quick effect, decrease spacing to two-thirds of the plant's mature spread (but not less than that).

SPACING TREES

Trees can also be spaced further apart or closer together than their mature spread, depending on the effect you're after. For example, if you want a grove, you may space your trees closer than the recommendations so canopies will grow together. (Slow-growing species may take decades to reach mature sizes.) Examine how the eventual size will affect your site, but design your landscape with moderate estimates of canopy size.

PERENNIALS

Perennials can be shown on your plan using the same method as you did for shrubs. This is the best way to get an accurate representation of where plants should go and how many will be needed. Scribble notes on the circles on your plan so you'll remember what plants they represent.

CALCULATING IRREGULAR BEDS

When it comes to calculating ground covers and any planting in irregularly shaped areas, use the following method. Roughly sketch 1-inch squares over the beds or lay your tracing paper over grid paper. Shade incomplete squares with pencil and include in your computation partial squares that together make a whole. Count the number of complete squares and multiply them by the number of square feet in each square. For example, a bed containing five complete squares on a 10-scale plan contains 500 square feet—5 squares times 100 (that's 10' × 10' for each square). Figure for all bed areas, including mulch and lawn areas.

The amount of ground cover you need will depend upon the spacing between plants. Different ground covers grow at different rates, so check with nurserymen or reference material to determine the proper spacing. If you're doing the work yourself, you can save money by setting out lots of small plants. But if you're paying for installation, you may spend more in labor costs than you would by purchasing fewer, larger plants. Refer to the chart below to select the appropriate planting factor. Multiply your square footage by the factor in the table. Round results up and use as a guide for pricing and purchasing ground cover.

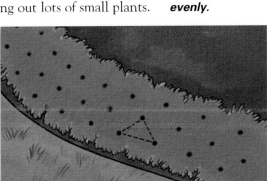

Use triangular spacing when you plant annual, perennial, and ground cover beds. The staggered formation will fill the bed space evenly.

CALCULATING GROUND COVER BASED ON TRIANGULAR SPACING

To calculate the number of plants you need to buy, look on the chart below for the space you want to leave between plants. Divide the total square footage of your ground cover bed by the corresponding denominator and round up.

Spacing between plants	Denominator
4"	.094
6"	.217
10"	.601
12"	.866
18"	1.95
24"	3.46
30"	5.41

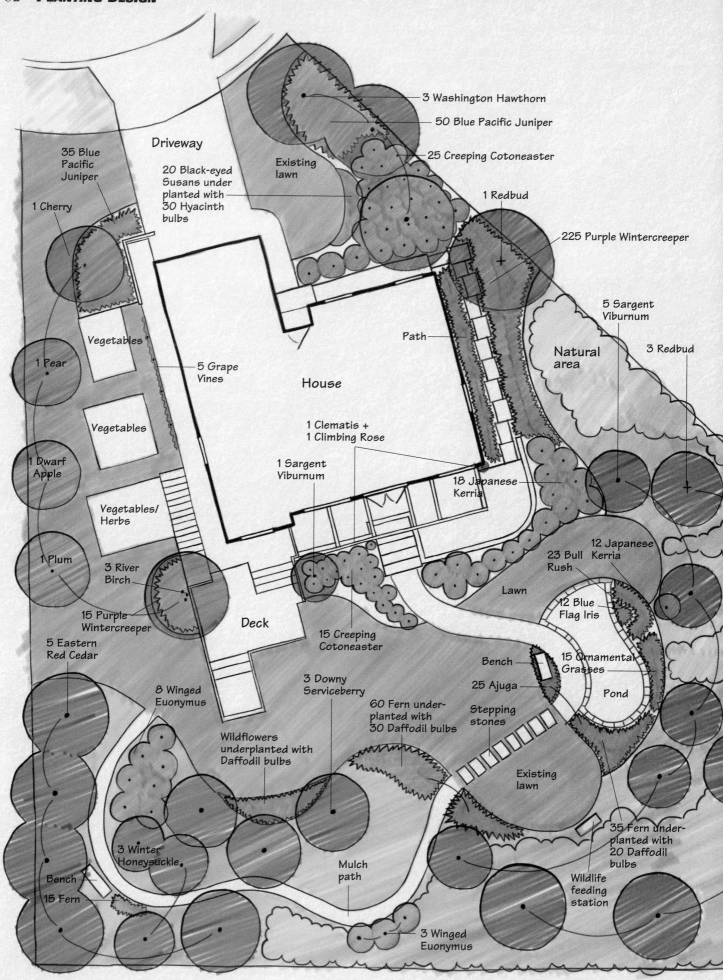

35 Blue Pacific Juniper

Driveway

1 Cherry

20 Black-eyed Susans under planted with 30 Hyacinth bulbs

Existing lawn

3 Washington Hawthorn

50 Blue Pacific Juniper

25 Creeping Cotoneaster

1 Redbud

225 Purple Wintercreeper

Vegetables

1 Pear

5 Grape Vines

Path

5 Sargent Viburnum

3 Redbud

Vegetables

Natural area

House

1 Dwarf Apple

1 Clematis + 1 Climbing Rose

1 Sargent Viburnum

18 Japanese Kerria

Vegetables/ Herbs

12 Japanese Kerria

23 Bull Rush

1 Plum

3 River Birch

15 Purple Wintercreeper

Deck

15 Creeping Cotoneaster

Lawn

12 Blue Flag Iris

5 Eastern Red Cedar

Bench

15 Ornamental Grasses

25 Ajuga

Pond

8 Winged Euonymus

3 Downy Serviceberry

Stepping stones

60 Fern under-planted with 30 Daffodil bulbs

Wildflowers underplanted with Daffodil bulbs

Existing lawn

35 Fern under-planted with 20 Daffodil bulbs

3 Winter Honeysuckle

Mulch path

Wildlife feeding station

Bench

15 Fern

3 Winged Euonymus

PLANTING PLAN

Though you may have been tempted to launch a landscape project by beginning with the planting plan, it's important that you have waited until now. Having worked your way sequentially through the design process, you now have much more information and tools that will make your plan complete and coordinated.

To make the plan itself, lay tracing paper over your master plan and trace outlines of hardscape, house, property lines, and the existing plants you want to keep. Lightly trace bed lines, too. (Make sure you're using your latest revision—you have likely made changes.) Lay this tracing over your planting schematic so you can see where you need to plant and the plant qualities you listed for each area.

As a result of all your research, you should have several specific plant names written next to each quality. Narrow these selections down as you prepare your planting plan. Remember to repeat some of the same plants throughout the beds or planting areas to create unity in your planting scheme.

Refer to your notes regarding plant spacing and check your concept diagram to ensure that your final plant selections are meeting the design goals you intended.

TREES FIRST

Draw trees on your planting plan first. Put a bold dot in a spot where you need to plant a tree. Take out your large circle template and select the size that corresponds to the spread of the tree at the scale of your drawing. Draw a quick circle around the dot to represent the canopy. It's okay if your tree circles overlap patios, driveways, decks, lawn, and shrub beds. Those overlaps will show you how the tree canopies will shade these areas. Remember, your template is a tool to help you sketch at the correct scale. It is not necessary to produce a professionally drafted plan.

BED LINES AND GROUPINGS

Adjust bed lines if necessary to accommodate your tree planting ideas. Next, refer to your planting schematic and divide beds into areas that represent different plant groupings. (Don't be afraid to alter an earlier plant choice.) Then determine the spacing for your plants and draw circles that touch each other, beginning and continuing along the bed lines. Each circle represents a mature or nearly mature plant. Draw a dot in the center of each circle; that will be where you're going to dig each planting hole. Shade the outline of all the plant groups.

Plants (circles) that you intend to scatter throughout a bed do not have to touch. For example, three accent plants set in a bed of ground cover would be shown as three separate circles. Instead of drawing tiny circles for ground cover, give the bed area a simple pattern to distinguish it from other areas.

REVISE AS YOU GO

Don't become so engrossed in drawing circles that you are unwilling to make mistakes and start again. You may need several layers of tracing paper to get your planting design just right. Remember, the design process is ongoing. You may refine bed lines, plant choices, and locations, and even hardscape as you work. Be sure to adjust other plans that may be affected by your changes. When you're finished, compile a list of plants used on your plan. Take a tally of quantities and sizes. Use this for estimating and shopping. Trace a second copy of your planting plan to take outside when you begin the installation of your dream landscape.

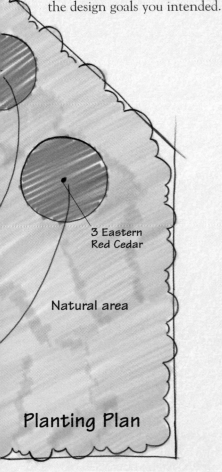

3 Eastern
Red Cedar

Natural area

Planting Plan

PLANNING FOR EASY
MAINTENANCE

WATERING

If there is a single common thread among all successful gardens, it is the availability of consistent moisture. Deciding how water will be delivered to your landscape is one of the most important elements of your maintenance plan.

Make watering easy on yourself; don't haul hoses. At a minimum, locate bibs on every side of the house and mount reels for separate hoses at each location.

Although quantity is important, consistency is almost as essential. If roots are allowed to dry out in between waterings, they are not as efficient at absorbing water the next time. Water regularly, preferably in the morning. The amount of water needed by plants in your landscape will determine how often you will need to water.

A typical lawn and shrub planting may require 1 inch of water per week, but vegetable and flower gardens that are packed with plants all competing for the same moisture may need up to 1½ inches per week. Some properties have a high water table that keeps the soil regularly moist; others with sandy soil may require more frequent and generous waterings to compensate for the rapid run-off. Needs vary in different regions of the country, too; check with your county cooperative extension to get specific recommendations for your area.

It's better to provide a greater quantity of water three times a week than a little bit every day. Greater quantities will soak in deeper and encourage deep root growth. Smaller quantities only keep the first few inches of the topsoil damp, encouraging shallow root growth.

CONSIDER CONSERVATION

Water conservation should be a concern of gardeners everywhere. Use whatever amount of water you need to keep gardens healthy and growing, but look for ways to conserve.

Watering in the morning gives plants the moisture they need to face the heat of the day. It also helps prevent fungal growth that may occur on foliage and mulch left damp overnight. Use a gentle spray to mimic rainfall; water long enough to soak roots.

Timers can be attached to spigots to turn water on regularly. This is always helpful, especially when you are gone for prolonged periods of time. Soaker hoses laid in planting beds allow water to seep through perforations to gently water roots.

Overhead watering loses more than 30 percent to evaporation. Whenever possible, use soaker hoses that deliver water directly to the soil and to plant roots. Soaker hoses are black, porous hoses made from recycled rubber and polyethylene. They have numerous tiny pores through which water weeps. You can design your own system with 'T' and elbow fittings. Lay the soaker hoses 2 feet apart through vegetable, rose, and flower gardens and around shrubs and trees. Cover the hoses with mulch for greater efficiency.

SOAKER PROBLEMS

Soaker hose systems have a few problems, but their remedies are easy. Fix periodic breaks or splits with a coupler and hose clamps. Prevent clogging with filters. Perhaps the worst problem is the potential for waste when water is not shut off. A forgotten sprinkler is hard to overlook, but soaker hoses can run unnoticed for quite a while.

There are two simple cures. The first is a common kitchen timer which you can set to ring at the end of your watering period. The second is an automatic timer that attaches between the hose and water source. Several models are available; some are driven by the water pressure going through the timer. More sophisticated—and more accurate—models are battery-powered. Some can be programmed to turn the water on and off on specified days of the week, as well as certain times of the day—the water-conservation answer for the gardener who must be away from home.

IRRIGATION SYSTEMS

Irrigation systems are the best—and, of course, the most expensive—option for watering. Some systems are homeowner do-it-yourself projects; intricate systems, however, may call for professional installation. You'll want to include a timing device to regulate the system throughout the week. Get one that can be set for early morning watering; that's when the water pressure is highest. Some systems have an override feature that prevents it from watering when it rains.

Irrigation systems can be custom designed with different sizes and types of sprinkler heads strategically placed in specific parts of your landscape. Such design delivers large amounts of water to large areas, such as lawns, but smaller amounts at ground level for planting beds.

Plan ahead for access through planting beds to your spigot. It's a good idea to build a gravel filled drainage well so dripping water won't make a muddy mess.

Pop-up irrigation heads are recessed until the water comes on, making them unnoticeable and easy to mow around. Some systems are do-it-yourself projects. For others, it's best to take your completed planting plan to a landscape architect or irrigation designer or contractor.

20 DROUGHT-TOLERANT PLANTS

LAWN GRASSES
Buffalograss
 (*Buchloe dactyloides*)
Blue gramagrass
 (*Bouteloua gracilis*)
Fairway crested wheatgrass
 (*Agropyron cristatum*
 'Ephraim')
Hard fescue
 (*Festuca longifolia*
 'Scaldis')
Canada bluegrass
 (*Poa compressa* 'Cannon'
 or 'Rubens')

TREES
Boxelder maple
 (*Acer negundo*)
Scotch pine
 (*Pinus sylvestris*)
Common hackberry
 (*Celtis
 occidentalis*)
Green ash
 (*Fraxinus
 pennsylvanica*)
Black Hill spruce
 (*Picea glauca* var. *densata*)
Colorado spruce
 (*Picea pungens*)
Ponderosa pine
 (*Pinus ponderosa*)
Bur oak
 (*Quercus macrocarpa*)

SHRUBS
Artemisia
 (*Artemisia* species)
Siberian pea-shrub
 (*Caragana arborescens*)
Silverberry
 (*Elaeagnus commutata*)
Alpine currant
 (*Ribes alpinum*)
Buffalo berry
 (*Shepherdia argentea*)
Threelobe spirea
 (*Spiraea trilobata*)
Soapwood
 (*Yucca glauca*)

MAINTAINING HEALTHY SOIL

Before you begin your maintenance plan, get to know your soil and become familiar with steps you can take to maintain its health.

MULCHING

Your maintenance plan should designate the mulching system you will use in your new landscape. Mulching is the practice of covering the surface of the soil with organic or inorganic material after all the planting is done. Organic mulches include wood chips, bark, grain hulls, mounds of hay, dried grass clippings, or pine needles (called pine straw in the South). Inorganic mulches, such as black plastic or layers of newspaper, can be covered with white marble chips or gravel.

Mulch helps newly planted beds look finished and dresses up existing beds. Mulch is essential for preserving moisture and helping prevent weed growth. When grading, make sure edges of planting beds are slightly lower than adjacent paving so mulch will not spill onto walkways and patios. Mulch should form a layer that is 2 to 3 inches thick. Do not pile mulch around trees and shrubs.

GOOD MULCHES

Many different organic materials make good mulch. It is important to see what is readily available in your area to cut costs and make it easier to replenish beds annually. Ground pine bark is preferable to large nuggets, which float and may wash away during a heavy downpour. Many nurseries are carrying shredded melaleuca as a substitute for shredded cypress to avoid cutting down native cypress stands. Pine straw and hay work well. Fine pebbles can do the job and help solve drainage problems, but they won't add organic matter to the soil. The following are all good organic mulches.

Redwood (small bark)
Mushroom compost
Rotted manures
Straw
Shredded tree leaves
Pine needles
Composted sawdust
Home compost
Pine straw
Cocoa bean shells
Rice hulls
Ground corn cobs

Inorganic mulches last longer but can be problematic. Gravel migrates into lawns and onto walkways and drives. Those lovely marble chips look dirty after a while. Plastic breaks down and is reduced to a thousand plastic chips.

Organic mulches are preferable (but need to be renewed more often). They improve the soil, with the help of earthworms. As the mulch degrades, the earthworms consume it. They deposit digested material in the form of castings deep in the soil where it will do the most good. If the soil around your foundation plantings is hard and dry, organic mulch will attract the worms, and they will repair and enrich the soil in only a few months.

FIVE FUNCTIONS

Mulch makes plants look nice. Mulch laid around trees, foundation shrubs, and garden plantings is like a frame on a picture; it makes the planting appear finished.

Applied around vertical elements, such as trees or poles, mulches make mowing easier.

Mulches help control weeds. They don't insure you'll have a weed-free garden, but the few that do come up will stand out against the mulch and they will pull more easily.

Mulch also reduces the amount of evaporation from the soil. With well-mulched soil, you'll use—and waste—less water.

Finally, organic mulching recycles products that might go into a landfill but instead become valuable landscape assets.

HOW MUCH TO ADD?

Two to three inches of mulch is sufficient. You will need to top it off every year or two as it degrades. If you are using mulch to stop erosion on a hillside and you don't have immediate plans to plant there, spreading 6 or more inches will inhibit erosion and dramatically improve the soil.

Some gardeners think the best combination is black plastic under organic mulch, but this, too, has disadvantages. The plastic remains intact longer because it is protected by the mulch on top. But the organic material can't enter the soil and improve it. Porous weed fabric, made of a nylon weave, is a better option than plastic, but be aware that weeds will grow on top of the fabric after it ages a year or two.

FERTILIZERS

Your earlier plans called for soil evaluation; now your maintenance plan should determine the type of fertilizers you will use.

Soils often contain many of the trace minerals and nutrients that plants need to grow. But you may need to add nitrogen, phosphorous, and potassium (N, P, and K on fertilizer labels). Fertilizers contain one or more of these elements in a variety of percentages. The numbers on all fertilizer labels list the percentages of these three elements for that particular formulation. For example a fertilizer rated as 5-10-5 contains 5 percent nitrogen, 10 percent phosphorous, and 5 percent potassium.

As a general rule, use high nitrogen fertilizers, such as a 10-6-4, for plants grown for their foliage (hedges and shade and evergreen trees) and high phosphorous fertilizers for plants grown for flowers, fruits, and vegetables. Always apply fertilizers according to label directions. More is not better! The amount recommended is the maximum you should apply. This is especially true of nitrogen. Too much nitrogen can burn and even kill plants.

INCORPORATING COMPOST

Don't overlook the opportunity to plan for a backyard composting center in your new landscape. Compost is the best soil amendment available to gardeners. No other single substance improves the texture, water retention, and drainage qualities of your soil better than compost. Compost, however, is relatively low in nutrients. Most compost measures at about 1-1-1 or less, so adding fertilizer still remains a must.

Dig compost at least 12 inches deep into vegetable and annual flower gardens in the spring, fall, and in between crops. Top dress perennial beds and trees and shrubs with compost. Then cover it with mulch.

MAKE YOUR OWN COMPOST

Anything that is organic—was once alive—will compost naturally. The goal is to do it with the least amount of smell and mess, and to avoid attracting vermin and neighborhood animals. Buy a system or construct a container that allows you to turn the material, add to it, and easily harvest it when it's done. The container you construct may be as simple as a snow fence or chicken wire bin; purchased systems can be as elaborate as a three-bin, pressure-treated wooden structure with galvanized wire sides. As you add to the mixture, pay attention to the balance between the fresh green vegetation and kitchen scraps—which account for most of the nitrogen—and the dried leaves, which account for most of the carbon. If your pile develops a foul smell, it needs more carbon. If it doesn't generate heat, it needs more nitrogen.

WATER-SOLUBLE FERTILIZERS

The most common fertilizers on the market are the water-soluble variety. These are mixed with water before application and can be used on landscape plants effectively. One of the easiest methods of application is with an in-hose sprayer—an excellent way for mid-season fertilizing of tightly packed flower beds and other hard-to-reach areas. One of the bonuses of using a water-soluble fertilizer is that the plants will be able to absorb the nutrients through the foliage as well as through the roots, giving them a "quick shot."

Always use the right fertilizer (granular or liquid) for the right type of plant and never overfertilize. Follow label directions exactly.

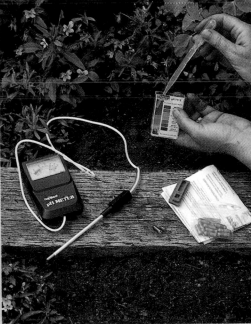

SOIL TESTING

Soil can be tested for its nutrient content as well as for its pH. The pH of a soil is a measure of its acidity or alkalinity. Soil pH is important because it affects the ability of plants to gather nutrients from the soil. Here's how to test your own. Gather a group of four to six tablespoon-sized samples of soil from the lawn (at a depth of 4 to 6 inches), another group from the vegetable garden, and so forth. Mix each group in separate brown paper bags and allow to dry. Test the soil with a good quality pH test kit (or send them to a soil testing laboratory) and correct the soil according to the test results.

Soil test kits are available from county extension agents. Knowing whether soil is acidic or alkaline will help you choose plants that thrive naturally in your garden. You can also add amendments to improve the pH as needed.

MOWING AND PRUNING

Mowing and pruning, of course, are regular chores for every landscape. If you're a gardener who doesn't like these chores, the simplest solution for you is to plant less lawn and plants that need pruning. But even if you enjoy the work, thoughtful design can make it easier.

Examine your plan. Consider the following ways of reducing mowing chores. One of the biggest favors you can do for yourself is to make sure lawn areas are relatively level and wide enough to be mowed easily.

Steep slopes and narrow grass strips are a headache. Plant banks and hillsides with ground cover and shrubs; do the same in shady areas or where tree roots make mowing difficult. Or create terraces with retaining walls (make sure access from one to another is easy with a mower). If your bed lines make strips that are less than a mower width, widen the grassy areas.

Grass that grows next to walls, fences, and trees is difficult to mow. So is lawn around stepping stones. Save time with design—add a mow strip at the foot of walls, mulch the base of trees, incorporate planting beds instead of grass, and recess stepping stones. To make mowing easier next to planting beds, cut V-trenches between lawns and garden areas.

Finally, think twice before clearing natural areas. Add trees or shrubs instead of creating large spaces you'll need to mow forever.

Keep pruning to a minimum by putting the right plant in the right place. Although it's important to know how tall and how wide a

Regular mowing is better for your lawn than allowing it to grow tall, then cutting it short to make the mowing last longer (as shown in this photo). Make sure you alternate mowing patterns so you don't end up with ruts and stripes in your lawn. When you need to add gasoline, move the mower to a paved area to avoid damaging fuel spills on your lawn.

plant will grow, it's equally important to know what form it will assume. Choose plants that meet your design intentions so you won't have to prune all the time to keep them in shape. Space plants far enough from paved areas to allow room for growth without crowding. Also keep your pruning on a schedule that conforms to the needs of the plant; a little done at the right time will save you a lot of effort later.

MAINTENANCE SCHEDULE FOR PLANTS

"Haircut" prune spring-blooming shrubs after bloom.
"Drastically" prune (more than one-third of plant) spring bloomers in the early spring.
Prune summer bloomers in the spring.
Deadhead spent flowers immediately.
Remove foliage of perennial flowers only after it turns yellow or brown.
Fertilize perennials when planting and when they first appear in the spring.
Fertilize annuals (including vegetables) when planting and throughout the season.
Apply pesticides; always follow directions.

CHOOSING PRUNING TOOLS

When choosing a pruning tool, consider the size of the branches you will be cutting. Long-handled loppers are necessary for cutting anything as large as your index finger. Hand pruners can be used for smaller stems. Use a pruning saw for branches that are ¾ inch in diameter or larger. Using the right tool will make clean cuts. Jagged cuts can encourage insect entry and damage.

MAINTAINING HEALTHY PLANTS AND WEEDING

The first step to maintaining healthy plants is to research the conditions in which they thrive. Plants have specific preferences for where they like to grow, and choosing the right plant for the right place will go a long way toward reducing its care.

Although it's not possible to create a specific environment for each plant, you can plan their locations now so you will grow them in the places they'll do best.

Locate plants that require full sun in areas receiving at least six to eight hours of sunlight a day (partial sun is defined as about four hours daily; shade means less than two hours of direct sun daily). In wet areas of the property, use plants that thrive when their feet are wet.

Consider building raised beds—even waist-high with supporting walls; they will save both time and reduce the toll that bending and stooping takes. And even if you don't raise your planting beds, consider their width and the space between them. Where possible design your beds so you can reach the middle from both sides for plant care chores and weeding. And plan to leave room between foundation plantings and the house for access.

Good air circulation is a must for preventing plant disease; plan your planting, especially that for trees, to allow enough space for air flow. Proper and timely pruning of roses and vines will keep the interior of the plants open and reduce conditions favoring disease. (Planning won't replace the need for inspection and intervention. Check your plants regularly and take appropriate steps to control any pests.)

Controlling weeds is one of the best ways to keep plants healthy. Weeds consume water and nutrients that desirable plants need. Pulling, cultivation, and tilling are all time-tested methods, but mulch is the greatest time saver of them all. A thick mulch cover reduces weed growth, makes pulling them easier, and helps retain moisture. Plan to use a preemergence herbicide to prevent germination of annual weeds such as crabgrass.

Cutting a V-trench with a shovel will discourage grass from growing into beds.

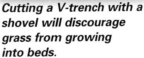

Hard surfaces make excellent edging. You can use a walkway to separate a planting bed from your lawn or add a brick mow strip as a divider.

Allowing a plant to grow in its natural form significantly reduces your maintenance efforts. Other than occasionally trimming stray branches, you won't have to prune. Plan ahead so the form and size of naturally shaped plants will fit into your landscape.

If you don't mind the work, include clipped hedges in your landscape for a neat, formal look. You can emphasize lines and delineate areas effectively with trimmed greenery. It's best to clip hedges starting early, instead of trying to transform mature plants into formal shapes.

MAINTAINING HARDSCAPES AND HARDWARE

Weeds often take advantage of space between brick or stones. If you don't have mortar between bricks and it's too late to place them tightly together, apply a systemic weed killer on a sunny day. Dig out dead weeds and fill cracks with topsoil. Seed with rye grass or fill with plugs of ground covers or herbs for attractive, low-growing plants within your walk.

Your maintenance schedule should include regular checkups for your hardscape and hardware, and your plan should include elements of design that makes their care much easier.

Some of the concerns discussed below include prevention; for others, remediation is unavoidable. In either case, it's wise to consider this information in the planning stages so you can save steps in the future.

When weeds and grass grow in the cracks of a path or patio, their roots can lift the paving. Then, when you pull the weeds, the roots will hang on to some soil or sand and leave voids that settle. Spraying the weeds will kill the plants but leave the roots and the soil undisturbed.

Algae is unsightly, dangerous, and potentially damaging to hardscape surfaces. Algae on a shady path can be very slippery; on decks and other wood surfaces, it can damage finishes. For algae-covered masonry surfaces, spray a 10 percent bleach solution and wait a week. You may have to repeat this process several times. Test an inconspicuous section of your deck with this remedy before you spray the whole area to make sure the bleach doesn't damage the surface.

To remove algae from your deck or other surfaces, pressure-wash the wood or apply a deck cleaning solution with a stiff brush. When it's completely dry, apply several coats of stain to protect the wood from water damage. You may need to thin tree canopies to allow more sunlight on your deck to keep it dry, discouraging algae growth. Make sure down spouts are not overflowing. You can also purchase effective moss and algae controls.

When the mortar between the joints of paths and patios begins to crumble and crack,

Repointing masonry is a good way to extend the life of brick walks and patios. When mortar becomes crumbly and loose, scrape it out and apply fresh mortar. Though time-consuming, repointing costs less than replacing masonry.

BASIC TOOLS FOR THE WELL-STOCKED TOOL SHED

Long-handled spade	Bow saw
Short-handled spade	Lawn spreader
Garden fork	Lawn mower
Narrow trowel	String trimmer
Wide trowel	Linseed oil (for
Hoe	wooden handles)
Lubricating oil	Sharpening file
Leaf rake	Long handled
Iron rake	trimming saw
Scissors-type	Garden shoes or
pruning shears	boots
Loppers	Gloves
Pruning saw	Chemical masks

it's important to repoint it as soon as possible. Cracks will allow water to erode the supporting soil or sand. And ice can lift and crack the heaviest of stones.

Mortared stone walls also fall victim to water and ice. Top the wall with a concrete cap or mortared stone to shed the rain and prevent pockets of water from accumulating inside. Or seal any mortared surface with a masonry sealer.

Decks should be stained or sealed regularly. If sealing hasn't been done in a while, you may have to remove the algae and old stain first with a power washer.

The right tools can make the difference between hard work and rewarding chores. Buy the best tools you can afford, and take care of them. In many cases, they will last a lifetime and become old friends. The first step to taking care of tools is to have a proper place to store them. A utility shed is ideal for this purpose. Arrange hangers on the wall and drawers and boxes so that every tool has its place. This will encourage you and the kids to put them away when you're done.

Keep all instruction manuals and warranty information in a designated drawer. This will be a great asset when you have to replace the string on your weed whacker or mix oil and gas for the chain saw for the first time in a while. In addition to garden tools, keep repair tools organized and handy. A set of socket wrenches, pliers, screwdrivers, and files are a must. Oil, grease, general lubricants, and boiled linseed oil should also be in your shed.

Storing your tools properly will dramatically increase their life. Rub the wooden handles of tools and wheelbarrows with a rag soaked in linseed oil to preserve the wood. Clean any soil and dirt from shovels, rakes, and other tools, and oil the metal parts. Sharpen not only pruning shears and clippers, but also shovels and hoes. Disassemble weed whackers, chain saws, and other machinery and clean thoroughly. Put your lawn mower away, conditioned for the spring. Sharpen the blade, change the plugs, points, and filters, if necessary, and clean and oil underneath the blade housing. Leave a full tank of gas over the winter to prevent rust, but add a fuel preservative to inhibit gumming. If you are storing gasoline in a container over the winter, add some fuel preservative to the container, as well.

Your lawn mower blade should be sharpened once or twice during the season to insure a clean cut on your grass.

Storage of pesticides and fertilizers is a little tricky. Fertilizers will last many years as long as they don't get damp. Don't let pesticides freeze. Keep them locked up.

TOOL CARE

Yard tools are an investment worth taking care of. Hang tools out of the weather to keep them dry and handy. A pegboard rack or specialty tool hangers can do the trick. You're more likely to get to work if you can quickly find what you need. Hanging tools is also a good way to keep them out of the reach of children.

Sharpen tools regularly to keep them effective. You're less likely to end up with sore muscles if pruners cut easily and shovels are sharp enough to dig through clay and roots. Dull tools require too much pressure to work, which can leave you stiff and leave plants damaged. Sharpen mower blades, too, for clean cuts with no stray sprigs left standing tall.

Always clean tools before storing them. Rinsing shovels in a bucket of water or scraping them in clean sand will extend their life by preventing rust. Squirt pruning tools with a stream of water after each use to avoid spreading disease from one plant to another. Oil them with a light coat after rinsing. Always rinse chemical containers.

HOW TO STORE AND CARE FOR CHEMICALS

Whether you use natural pest controls and fertilizers or the synthesized variety, all sprays, dusts, and granules are chemical compounds. As such, they are subject to chemical change and breakdown of key components. These changes are caused by age, temperature, moisture, and sunlight. Freezing almost always damages pesticides and liquid fertilizers. Storage in garden sheds over the winter in cold climates will render them useless. Dry fertilizers, on the other hand, have a very long life if kept dry. Keep all garden chemicals locked up. Ironically, many organic pesticides are as toxic as are their synthesized cousins.

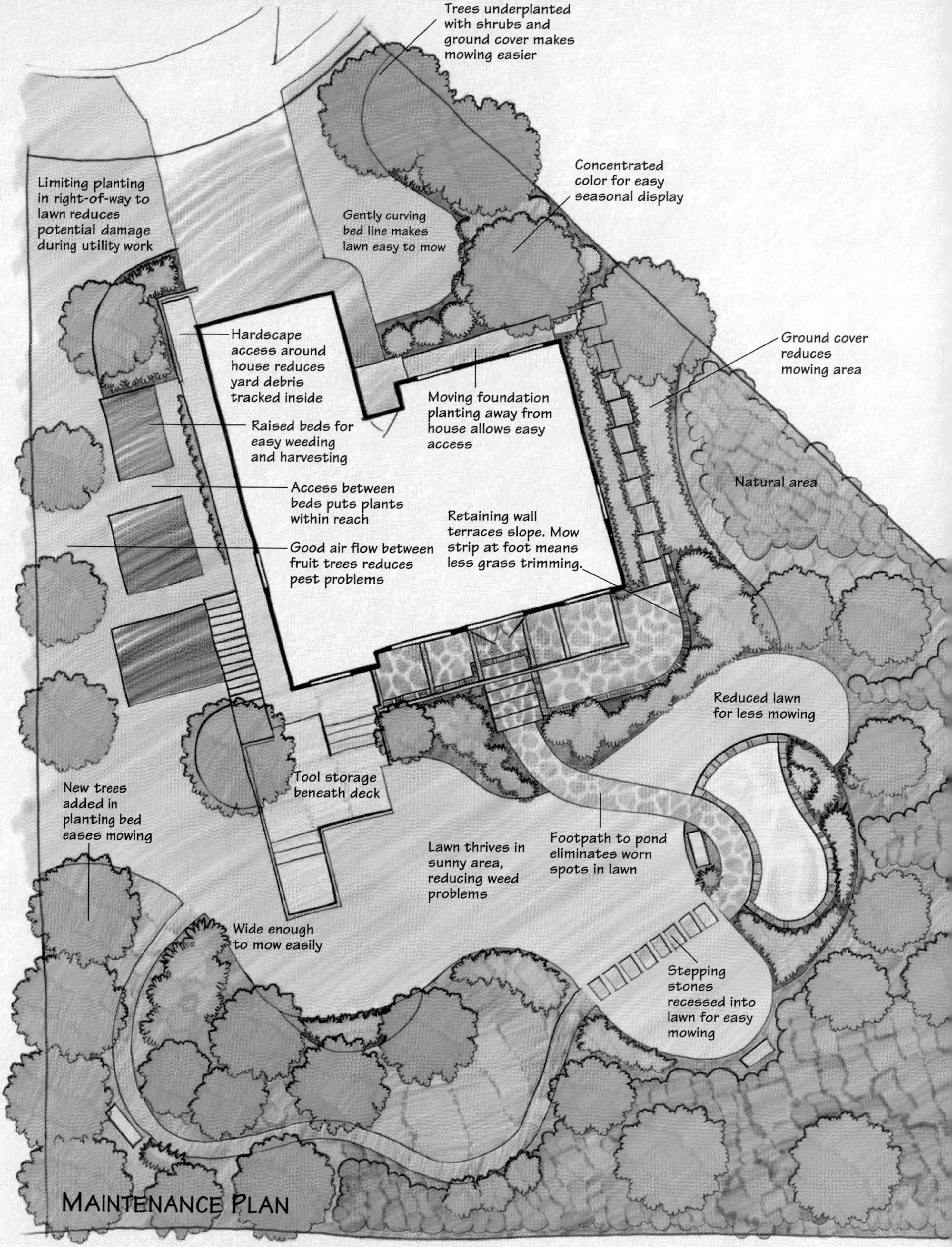

Trees underplanted with shrubs and ground cover makes mowing easier

Concentrated color for easy seasonal display

Limiting planting in right-of-way to lawn reduces potential damage during utility work

Gently curving bed line makes lawn easy to mow

Hardscape access around house reduces yard debris tracked inside

Moving foundation planting away from house allows easy access

Ground cover reduces mowing area

Raised beds for easy weeding and harvesting

Natural area

Access between beds puts plants within reach

Retaining wall terraces slope. Mow strip at foot means less grass trimming.

Good air flow between fruit trees reduces pest problems

Reduced lawn for less mowing

New trees added in planting bed eases mowing

Tool storage beneath deck

Footpath to pond eliminates worn spots in lawn

Lawn thrives in sunny area, reducing weed problems

Stepping stones recessed into lawn for easy mowing

Wide enough to mow easily

MAINTENANCE PLAN

MAINTENANCE PLAN

Maintenance is the part of landscaping you may not want to think about. After all, planting flowers is more fun than pulling weeds. But it pays to consider maintenance before you install your new landscape. Prepare a maintenance plan similar to this one to identify improvements you can implement now to make your life easier later.

Take into consideration the forms of maintenance discussed in this chapter: watering, mulching, fertilizing, composting, mowing, pruning, treating plants for disease or pests, weeding, maintaining your hardscape, and storing and caring for tools.

Your maintenance plan should address all of these areas and consider their interaction.

Planting smart will eliminate many maintenance problems. Raising vegetable and flower beds makes planting, weeding, and harvesting easier with less bending. Ground cover planted in difficult-to-mow areas can reduce your yard work time for years to come.

Careful selection of mulch will reduce time spent weeding. Applying pre-emergence herbicide at the right times will help, too.

Place foundation plantings away from the house for easy access behind them for a hose bib as well as general pruning and fertilizing.

Well-planned storage access will reduce steps and frustration later. Careful placement of trees can reduce pest problems.

Install hose bibs on all sides of the house with separate hoses available to each; use hose reels for quick retraction.

This is also the time to consider traffic flow; the access you provide in your landscape can create maintenance problems or solve them. Inadequate circulation routes through your yard will result in worn paths

through lawns and shortcuts taken through beds. Make sure any walkways follow logical routes. Create pathways everywhere you travel often, such as the trash area, the pond, the utility area. Masonry or gravel pathways cut down on the amount of dirt tracked into the house.

Widen the intersection of walkways to form landings, especially when connecting to other paved areas such as driveways, parking courts, patios, and streets. Landings form transitions from larger paved areas to smaller ones. This prevents people from cutting across the corners of planting beds. Landings also provide places for people to pause in the landscape as they greet one another or say good-bye; providing a paved surface for this purpose makes your landscape welcoming.

Considering how you will take care of your landscape is the key to enjoying the outdoor areas of your property as much as the indoors.

Shovel-cutting a V-trench between planting beds and lawn will help keep the areas neatly separated.

Add new trees within planting beds and consider extending existing beds to surround trunks with ground cover or shrubs. This improves the look of your lawn, as grass does not generally thrive directly beneath trees. And it makes mowing easier.

When grass grows adjacent to a vertical surface, add a brick mow strip at the base of the wall. This gives mower wheels a hard surface and eliminates a shaggy, hard-to-mow strip of grass beside the wall. Or, consider adding a planting bed beside the wall to separate the lawn area.

Preserving natural area means less yard to maintain

THE USDA PLANT HARDINESS ZONE MAP OF NORTH AMERICA

Plants are classified according to the amount of cold weather they can handle. For example, a plant listed as hardy to zone 6 will survive a winter in which the temperature drops to minus 10° F.

Warm weather also influences whether a plant will survive in your region. Although this map does not address heat hardiness, in general, if a range of hardiness zones are listed for a plant, the plant will survive winter in the coldest zone as well as tolerate the heat of the warmest zone.

To use this map, find the location of your community, then match the color band marking that area to the zone key at left.

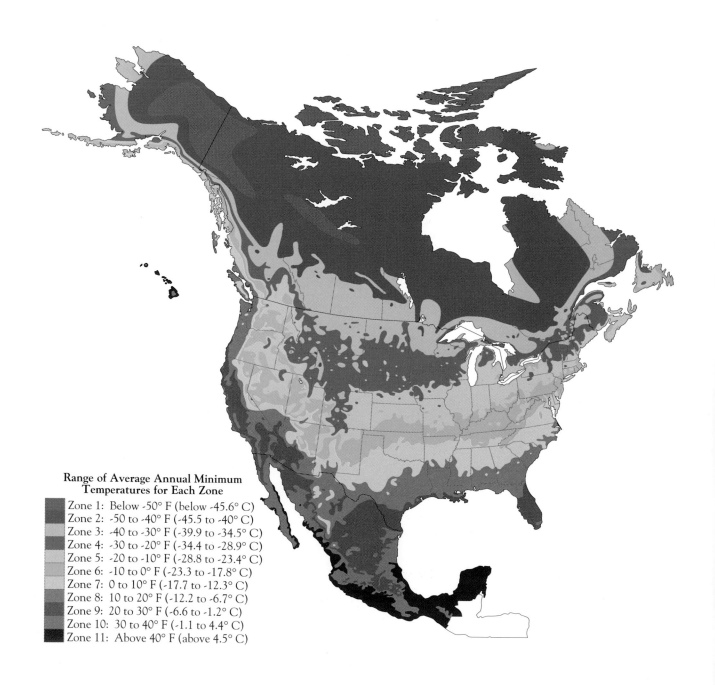

Range of Average Annual Minimum Temperatures for Each Zone

Zone 1: Below -50° F (below -45.6° C)
Zone 2: -50 to -40° F (-45.5 to -40° C)
Zone 3: -40 to -30° F (-39.9 to -34.5° C)
Zone 4: -30 to -20° F (-34.4 to -28.9° C)
Zone 5: -20 to -10° F (-28.8 to -23.4° C)
Zone 6: -10 to 0° F (-23.3 to -17.8° C)
Zone 7: 0 to 10° F (-17.7 to -12.3° C)
Zone 8: 10 to 20° F (-12.2 to -6.7° C)
Zone 9: 20 to 30° F (-6.6 to -1.2° C)
Zone 10: 30 to 40° F (-1.1 to 4.4° C)
Zone 11: Above 40° F (above 4.5° C)

INDEX

METRIC CONVERSIONS

U.S. Units to Metric Equivalents			Metric Units to U.S. Equivalents		
To Convert From	Multiply By	To Get	To Convert From	Multiply By	To Get
Inches	25.4	Millimeters	Millimeters	0.0394	Inches
Inches	2.54	Centimeters	Centimeters	0.3937	Inches
Feet	30.48	Centimeters	Centimeters	0.0328	Feet
Feet	0.3048	Meters	Meters	3.2808	Feet
Yards	0.9144	Meters	Meters	1.0936	Yards
Square inches	6.4516	Square centimeters	Square centimeters	0.1550	Square inches
Square feet	0.0929	Square meters	Square meters	10.764	Square feet
Square yards	0.8361	Square meters	Square meters	1.1960	Square yards
Acres	0.4047	Hectares	Hectares	2.4711	Acres
Cubic inches	16.387	Cubic centimeters	Cubic centimeters	0.0610	Cubic inches
Cubic feet	0.0283	Cubic meters	Cubic meters	35.315	Cubic feet
Cubic feet	28.316	Liters	Liters	0.0353	Cubic feet
Cubic yards	0.7646	Cubic meters	Cubic meters	1.308	Cubic yards
Cubic yards	764.55	Liters	Liters	0.0013	Cubic yards

To convert from degrees Fahrenheit (F) to degrees Celsius (C), first subtract 32, then multiply by 5/9.

To convert from degrees Celsius to degrees Fahrenheit, multiply by 9/5, then add 32.